The Poetics and Politics
of the Veil in Iran

The Poetics and Politics of the Veil in Iran

An Archival and Photographic Adventure

By Azadeh Fatehrad

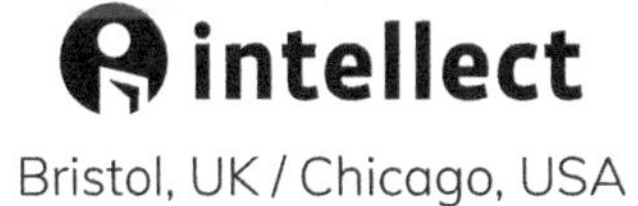

Bristol, UK / Chicago, USA

First published in the UK in 2019 by
Intellect, The Mill, Parnall Road, Fishponds, Bristol, BS16 3JG, UK

First published in the USA in 2019 by
Intellect, The University of Chicago Press, 1427 E. 60th Street,
Chicago, IL 60637, USA

A catalogue record for this book is available from the British Library.

Every effort has been made to trace copyright holders and to obtain their permission
for the use of copyright material. The author apologizes for any errors or omissions
and would be grateful if notified of any corrections that should be incorporated in
future reprints or editions of this book.

Copy editor: MPS Technologies
Cover designer: Aleksandra Szumlas
Cover image: Azadeh Fatehrad (2015),
Departure series. Photograph. Tehran.
Production manager: Naomi Curston
Typesetting: Contentra Technologies

Print ISBN: 978-1-78938-126-9
ePDF ISBN: 978-1-78938-128-3
ePUB ISBN: 978-1-78938-127-6

Printed and bound by Severn, UK

To find out about all our publications, please visit
www.intellectbooks.com.
There, you can subscribe to our e-newsletter,
browse or download our current catalogue,
and buy any titles that are in print.

This is a peer-reviewed publication.

This book is dedicated first to the women of my country of birth, Iran – with all your curiosity to search for our hidden history, whether inside or outside Iran, you have been a great inspiration for my resistance, strength and love.
Second, to the women of my adopted country of the UK, to your observations, doubts and generous support that have provided the nurturing platform for the creation of this book.

Contents

About the Book

The publication *The Poetics and Politics of the Veil in Iran: An Archival and Photographic Adventure* written by the Iranian born and London-based artist and curator Azadeh Fatehrad is a photographic–poetic meditation uncovering Iran's feminist history.

The chance discovery of a photograph taken in Teheran on 8 March 1979 of women marching in the streets in protest against the introduction of the compulsory Islamic dress code marks the starting point for Azadeh Fatehrad's journey as a diasporic artist in search of her own history. Through her research she uncovers more about the spontaneous uprising of 8 March 1979 and the complex history of feminism in Iran in the twentieth and twenty-first centuries.

The lives of women in Iran are explored across social, political and aesthetical contexts of veiling, unveiling and re-veiling. At the heart of the publication is the creation of an imaginary space of self-representation that responds, in poetic photographs and writing, to the legacy of the Iranian Revolution on the representation of women in photography, literature and film. The text and images move adeptly between the documentary, the analytical and the personal to create an accessible and theoretically nuanced visual narrative that rewires history and scholarly possibility.

The Poetics and Politics of the Veil in Iran: An Archival and Photographic Adventure demonstrates how forgotten archives can be reclaimed and used creatively to inspire new conversations and imaginaries of resistance. It offers a new form of evidence drawn from practice-based research that is academic, artistic and activist.

Preface

During my master's studies at London's Chelsea College of Arts, I attended a book launch by the German artist Sandra Schäfer, who was a visiting artist at Chelsea over the summer of 2009. When I flicked through the pages of Sandra's book, *Kabul/Tehran 1979ff* (2006), I encountered an astonishing image of women in my country in 1979. I was instantly fascinated by the image, and asked Sandra what she knew about it. She replied that the photographer was actually sitting in the audience. That was my first contact with Hengameh Golestan, one of the pioneers of photojournalism in Iran. Golestan's photograph became the origin – or starting point – of my project.

Here in London, for the first time I learned about the missing part of my own history, namely the uprising of 8 March 1979 when women took to the streets of Tehran in protest against the compulsory dress code. Golestan's photograph had opened a door onto the complex history of my own country, which is largely inaccessible to me back home.

Golestan's photograph thus became the emotional core of my project, and my research started to form around it as I acquired and made my way through piles of books about the history of Iran and Iranian feminism as well as texts about different cultural forms that, in one way or another, relate to representations of the veiled woman: for instance writings on Iranian cinema and photography, on literature and poetry, writings on architecture and gardens that talk about notions of protection and privacy. The resulting text is an assemblage of insights and references connected by the image of the veiled woman in Iran's history, in an attempt to express complex, ambivalent and ambiguous relationships to the veil as a symptom of an oppressive regime. In other words, I examine the effect of historical imposition of the wearing of the veil on the lives of women in terms of art, film, photography, literature and so on. I try to transform the received idea of what the veil is for Iranian women into a different kind of cultural form or object. I should note here that veiling (covering, *hijab*) in modern Iran refers to the headscarf and accompanying garments, as well as the veil (*chador*) itself. In fact, a mixture of attire can be seen on the streets. Since the focus of this project is modern Iran, the word is used to refer to both forms throughout.

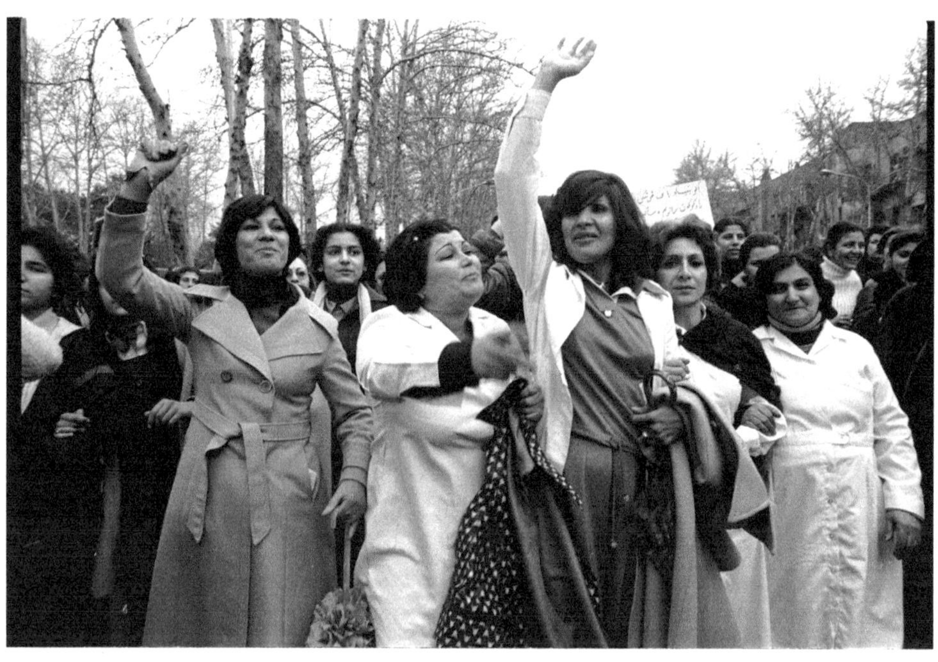

FIGURE 1: Hengameh Golestan, *Untitled* (Witness '79 series). © Hengameh Golestan.

Introduction

The act of covering has been an interesting and noticeable feature in the history of Iran. Interestingly, the compulsory unveiling and compulsory wearing of the veil to hide the hair and body of women has been introduced and repealed many times throughout Iran's history, beginning with Reza Shah's 1936 ban on the head-scarf and *chador* as part of his secularizing project.[1] This position is, of course, in stark contrast to what occurred some 40 years later when, following the 1979 Revolution, Ruhollah Khomeini reversed this decision and decreed that women should now cover their heads. During the twentieth century in Iran, the meaning of *hijab* went through several transformations. Unveiled women symbolized the secular and westernized regime of Mohammad Reza Shah Pahlavi. 'Wrapped in a black chador', these women became icons of the Islamic Revolution and, two decades later, their more relaxed, colourful and vibrant *hijabs* became the symbol of a new era of progress and reform in the Islamic Republic.

My project arose from an important and provocative historical image (Figure 1). This photograph was taken by the Iranian photographer Hengameh Golestan on the morning of 8 March 1979, following Khomeini's announcement of the compulsory covering. It shows a group of women marching in the streets of Tehran, taking part in a 100,000 strong protest of both men and women against the compulsory *hijab*.[2] Soon after the Revolution there were rumours of plans for the reintroduction of the *hijab,* and the abolition of several women's rights that had previously been protected by the Family Protection Act, the reason being that they were seen as 'against Islam'.[3] The photo intrigued me to the point that I wanted to find out more about it, to find out more about myself and the women of my society. The demonstration lasted for five days and ended when some violence was committed against the protesters by the revolutionary guards mobilized by the mullahs. The French group Pratique, Politique et Psychanalyse also documented the protests using a 16mm camera, and conducted interviews with the demonstrators. This led to the joint production of a 13-minute short film entitled *Mouvement de Libération des Femmes Iraniennes*: *Année Zéro,* which serves as the only video evidence of that historical moment.[4] At this juncture, it should be emphasized that my project is not about the *hijab* as an Islamic or political icon in itself; rather I am interested in approaching this act of imposing the covering on women as an opportunity to reflect on the imaginary dimension of veiling and unveiling.

Walter Benjamin recommends that the historian, rather than seeking to portray the past 'as it really was' (an unattainable ideal, in any event), should 'actualize' the epoch or event, with an eye towards its contemporary relevance.[5] Benjamin uses the word 'indirection' to express the effect of a past event as opposed to the event itself. It is important to note that indirection is not abstraction, but rather an expanded and wider area of cultural context, politics, visual culture and representation that can be applied to any event in history.

For me, 'indirection' was not a word that could be easily translated into Farsi. Indeed, I looked through several dictionaries to find an appropriate definition that I could use. For example, I discovered that in computer programming, indirection is the ability to reference something using a name, reference or container instead of the value itself; however, in military terminology, indirect fire refers to fire delivered at a target that is not itself used as a point of aim for the weapons or the person who fires them. All of these varied but related definitions have contributed to my understanding of how the notion of indirection can apply to this research – how instead of focusing solely on a single past event (i.e. 8 March 1979), I can more usefully analyse both it and its effects by looking at the entire time period before, during and after the event and the media that emerged from it. In other words, by looking at the history of feminism, by considering women's journals and publications, the history of photography, archival photographs and video material in both domestic and non-domestic settings, and by studying video footage of feature movies and the visual representation of the body in them, this project can take an indirect look at 8 March 1979, the events that led up to that date and the effects it had and continues to have to this day.

In my project, I am looking at the object of repression (the veil) in the history of Iran through a perspective of 'indirection', i.e. from a particular position of fascination and envy. I am suggesting a dimension of beauty and desire. Even though for western readers it might be more comfortable were I to follow the familiar discourse of condemning the *hijab* and standing defiantly against the compulsory dress code, and whilst I do naturally recognize the extent of the oppression that exists in Iran and am personally very much against the enforcement of any dress code, the specific aim of my research is to explore the affective and imaginary dimensions of the acts of covering and uncovering.

Taking my cue from Benjamin, my interest in an epoch or a past event and its effects (here the 1979 Revolution and the Women's Uprising against the compulsory dress code it provoked on 8 March 1979) is to enable me to find its relevance in the contemporary society we are living in today. The uprising has created a kind of iconic metaphorical 'monument' in the history of feminism in Iran, which should be remembered and preserved forever for all Iranian women. Benjamin himself uses the term *Aufheben*,[6] which refers to the process of historical material being referred to within a contemporary context, something that serves to preserve and even elevate the original 'monument' in the current time. Departing from its original time is to 'cancel' the real event, while by referring to it in contemporary time is to give it attention – a new life.

Aside from historical books such as *From Darkness into Light* (1980) and *Rethinking Global Sisterhood* (2007) that have helped to clarify the sequence of Iranian history for me, there have been several other sources that have enriched my project and influenced my journey through it, for instance *Things I've Been Silent About: Memories* (2008), *Reading Lolita in Tehran* (2003) and *Lipstick Jihad* (2005). I have also drawn on artists' works including Shirin Neshat's photographs and videos, and Marjane Satrapi's *Persepolis* animation (2000), as well as the work of inspiring filmmakers such as Manijeh Hekmat and Rakhshan Bani-E'temad.[7] Additionally, from my own personal experience of living for 26 years in Iran, I have many personal thoughts and observations to share about society in post-revolutionary Iran; it is, in fact, this first-hand experience that has continued to motivate me through this research.

> *For every image of the past*
> *that is not recognised by the present*
> *as one of its own concerns*
> *threatens to disappear irretrievably.*

Gottfried Keller[8]

NOTES

1. Ali Razi, *Tarih-I-Mofassal-I-Iran* (*The Complete History of Iran*) (Tehran: Eghbal and Shorakae Publication, 1956), 659–64.

2. Haideh Daragahi and Nina Witoszek, 'Anti-Totalitarian Feminism? Civic Resistance in Iran', in *Civil Society in the Age of Monitory Democracy*, Studies on Civil Society, ed. Lars Trägårdh, Nina Witoszek and Bron Taylor (Oxford: Berghahn Books, 2013), 23–54.

3. Ibid., 46.

4. Pratique, Politique et Psychanalyse (Michele Moulder, Sylvia Boiasuna, Claudine Mular and Sylven Rey), *Mouvement de Libération des Femmes Iraniennes: Année Zero*, France, 1979, YouTube, last modified 20 April 2015, https://www.youtube.com/watch?v=ul-JwXHji6f4.

5. Walter Benjamin and Hannah Arendt, *Illuminations: Theses on the Philosophy of History*, trans. Harry Zohn (London: Schocken Books, 1969), 263.

6. Translation: 'To preserve, to elevate, to cancel'. Benjamin and Arendt, *Illuminations*, 263–66.

7. Badr ol-Moluk Bamdad and Nasin Rahimieh, *From Darkness into Light: Women's Emancipation in* Iran, Costa Mesa: Mazda Publishers, 1980; Nima Naghibi, *Rethinking Global Sisterhood: Western Feminism and Iran*, Minneapolis: University of Minnesota Press, 2007; Azar Nafisi, *Reading Lolita in Tehran*, New York: Random House Inc., 2003; Azar Nafisi, *Things I've Been Silent About:* Memories, London: Penguin Random House, 2008; Azadeh Moaveni, *Lipstick Jihad: A Memoir of Growing up Iranian in America and American in* Iran, London: Public Affairs Publishing, 2006; Shirin Neshat and Shoja Azari, *Women Without Men*, DVD, USA: IndiePix Films, 2009; Shirin Neshat, *Women of* Allah, New York: Distributed Art Pub Inc., 1999; Marjane Satrapi and Vincent Paronnaud, *Persepolis*, DVD, France: Celluloid Dreams, 2000; Manijeh Hekmat, *Zendān-e Zanān* (*Women's Prison*), Iran: Bamdad Film, 2002; Rakhshan Bani-E'temad, *Kharej az Mahdudeh* (*Off Limits*), Iran: Filmsazan Cooperation, 1986; Rakhshan Bani-E'temad, *Narges*, Iran: Arman Films, 1992; Tahmineh Milani, *Do zan* (*Two Women*), Iran: Arman Film, 2009.

8. Benjamin and Arendt, *Illuminations*, 266.

Chapter One

1.1 Iran in 1936

To understand how much women had struggled before the Iranian Revolution, it is necessary to understand the reasons behind the violent uprising in response to the compulsory dress code of 1979. It had nothing to do with how they would look; rather, it reminded them of the backwardness and narrow-mindedness that they had fought so hard to get rid of, and the knowledge and independence that they had secured for themselves. They feared the hidden curtains that could once again make women useless and invisible. The women of Iran benefited from the changes that occurred under the reigns of the two Pahlavi monarchs (1925–79), Reza Shah and Mohammad Reza Pahlavi, in that they educated women and enabled them to enter the workforce. At the same time, there was considerable debate about the loss of tradition that modernity inevitably caused. The most important achievements for women during this time were perhaps securing the right to vote and seeing the passing of the Family Protection Law, both of which occurred around 1965.

It was 1925 when the Pahlavi dynasty started with Reza Shah Pahlavi (Reza Shah) as its first monarch. Reza Shah's vision for development 'included a citizenry that looked modern: men and women should dress in European style clothing, and women should appear in public without head covering'.[9] For a traditional society like Iran in which the use of the *chador* and modest clothing more generally dates back to at least the tenth century, this was a controversial step.

Between 1925 and 1936, Iran moved slowly towards modernization and a ban on traditional clothing. For more details, please refer to section 1.3 of this book related to the feminist history of Iran. It is, however, important to note that at that point there was already a small group of educated upper-class women such as Sadighe Dowlatabadi and Forough Shahab who had been active in setting up a handful of girls' schools and had already taken off their veil in public. This was alongside public figures such as Qamar-ol-Moluk Vaziri (1905–59), commonly known as Qamar, who was among the first women of her time to sing in public in Iran unveiled.

Badr ol-Moluk Bamdad calls the first Pahlavi monarch 'the Daybreak', and points to the 'momentous decree' delivered by the Shah on 7 January 1936, which banned the veil in public. On this day, Reza Shah attended a graduation ceremony at the University of Tehran and gave a powerful speech in support of women more generally.[10] In it, he encouraged women to be more active in society, considering them to be valued members, in particular stating that he wanted to see more women being educated. He believed that since women made up half of the Iranian population, their education would not only benefit them but also society as a whole.[11] He set out a vision for the future in which women were as active and powerful as men, giving them a higher status than they had ever enjoyed before. At this point, it seemed that Iranian women would emerge out of a situation where they had been kept in ignorance to one where they would become enlightened. In fact, following the ceremony, Reza Shah actually changed the rules regarding women's attire in public, imposing a western-style dress code of skirt and blouse while banning the veil or, indeed, any type of *hijab*.

Following Reza Shah's decree, any woman found covered in public was to be forcibly uncovered. One must remember that for many years previously, women had been covered; this sudden change was perceived by some as an act of violence against women. Indeed, feminists like Badr ol-Moluk Bamdad noted the verbal and physical harassment that veiled women were subjected to as Reza Shah's soldiers forcibly unveiled them. As a result, the Act of Unveiling (1936) ultimately ensured that women who had spent their entire lives wearing the veil would remain in the private confines of their homes since, for them, walking the street unveiled was tantamount to walking the street naked.[12] Other women decided to wear a loose cloak (manteau) and headscarf (*rusari*), which is the early version of the contemporary fashion seen in Tehran today.[13]

After this seminal day in Iranian history, women became policed by men, and their bodies became a site of enforcement. This situation is very similar to contemporary Iran, except that now, as a result of Khomeini's decree, women must cover themselves. This was the point at which he consolidated his power and effectively turned Iran into an Islamic state. Whoever is in power, it seems that the woman's body repetitively becomes the site of state control.

Nevertheless, despite the level of violence and aggression surrounding the Act of Unveiling, the dominant feminist response at the time was celebratory. It was seen as such an important milestone that Reza Shah made 7 January 'National Women's Day', replacing 8 March International Women's Day. In essence, Reza Shah was modernizing the country by destroying the boundaries between the *andaroni* (the private and inner domain) and the *bironi* (the public and outer domain). Women who were kept inside their homes, away from society and outside of public places, perceived the street as a dangerous and disconnected space (*namahram*). In order to maintain their safety and modesty they had to be kept away from this domain. While opposition to the veil from female activists and grassroots organizations during this time was one thing, armed police pulling the veil off women's heads in the street and being given a free reign to insult and humiliate veiled women as they wished was a completely different matter.

Following Reza Shah's controversial decision, women were forced to appear in the street as they would at home, that is, uncovered. In addition, they were meant to be as comfortable on the street as they were inside their homes. In an instant, notions of 'indoor' and 'outdoor', and the boundary between them, essentially dissolved following the unveiling decree.

Alternatively, this act can be seen as a kind of widening of the boundaries of the domestic to the public. One of Reza Shah's aims in passing the Act of Unveiling was in fact to democratize gender roles, in imitation of the western model, by unveiling women and encouraging mixed social gatherings. Prior to this decision, outside the home was a male-dominated area; only a very limited number of women were to be found in places such as cafes, public places, the workplace, educational settings and shops. The Act of Unveiling thus forced women to become active participants in life outside the home, for example through them visiting shops, entering schools, joining the workforce and generally being outside the home in the same way as men. In this way, women gradually became more independent and participated alongside men in society, meaning that society became a more balanced and mixed-gender environment. Because of Reza Shah's decision, 'outside the home' really did become a place for both men and women.

1.2 The Hijab in Iran

The *hijab* stands for modest clothing, and is a mark of a woman's social and economic status. In Farsi, *poshesh* ('clothing') derives from the verb *pushidan*, meaning to cover up or conceal from view, whereas the English term 'dress' refers, among other things, to decorating or adorning. During the Qajar dynasty, which ruled Iran from 1789 to 1925, many women wore *chador*. The *chador* ('tent' in Persian), which is made of a single, large semicircle of fabric, dates back to at least the tenth century.[14] Before 1936, middle- and upper-class urban women would wear full-length, head-to-toe clothing, and occasionally even an additional face covering called a *pichih*. The *hijab* for peasant and tribal women who worked mostly in the fields consisted of a colourful *rusari* ('headscarf') and loose clothing, which provided them with more freedom of movement than the floor-length *chador* and, therefore, greater comfort. *Sharm*, referring to a combination of charm and shame, connotes modesty, timidity and being soft-spoken; this notion remains one of the most valued qualities in a traditional Iranian woman. At the turn of the century, the more covered a woman was, and the more *sharm* she displayed in her behaviour and demeanour, the higher her social status was deemed to be.[15]

In 1941, the son of Reza Shah, Mohammad Reza Pahlavi (Mohammad Reza Shah), took over the throne. It was during his time that the conflict between traditional and religious, especially in so far as it related to women's dress, became particularly heated. In a religious context, the clergy or religious leaders have the power to issue a *fatwa* (a legal opinion) that Muslims must then follow and this is something the religious leaders in Iran did indeed practise during Mohammad Reza Shah's reign. For instance, in 1948, they issued a *fatwa* forbidding women from shopping while unveiled. The veil was, of course, still banned, yet many women chose to follow the *fatwa* and wore a veil to the shops. Therefore, Mohammad Reza Shah had to relax the enforcement of uncovering; he did continue to develop and modernize the country, including through a series of reforms known as the White Revolution in the 1960s and 1970s, but the banned veil had to be abandoned.[16]

Therefore, women were allowed to wear what they wanted again; hence, the hierarchy of women was somewhat eroded during the reign of Mohammad Reza Shah and unexpected forms of fashion, such as a short *chador* with high heels emerged, as revealed by videos in found archival footage depicting the lives of women in Tehran in the 1940s. One question that arises out of this is: *to what extent can fashion express an oppressive or liberated social condition?* Through these mixed fashion statements, it can be seen that middle- and upper-class urban women largely remained unveiled while traditional working-class women returned to wearing the *hijab*, although the form of *hijab* changed, since there was no longer a specific face covering or *pichih*, and some women returned to wearing the floor-length/short *chador* while others chose to wear the *rusari*. It should be noted that at this time it would not have been possible for a covered woman to have been employed in government. For the younger generation who had been brought up without the veil, the headscarf was generally considered unfashionable and a sign of backwardness and devout religiosity, all of which they were keen to distance themselves from. In summary, veiled and unveiled women were thus constantly moving between the interior and exterior, the personal and political, the western and the eastern.[17]

During this era, mid-twentieth century, slowly but surely, progress was made in terms of women's rights and status in society of Iran, but this progress was not consistent. For instance, whilst women readily had access to birth control pills and abortions, they still needed written permission from their husbands to travel abroad.[18] Reza Shah and, later, Mohammad Reza Pahlavi pushed through quick dramatic changes without any real platform that would allow women to negotiate their life outside of the home. On the surface, these changes might appear progressive, but the core structure was not stable and much was still needed to be done for women's rights. Under the iron rule of Reza Shah, the judiciary was secularized in 1931, but family law was left to the jurisdiction of the clergy and the dictate of Sharia law. This said, one great achievement during Mohammad Reza Shah's reign was the passing of the Family Protection Law in 1967, which set up special courts to deal with family law matters and put useful safeguards in place with regard to the minimum marriageable age, divorce and child custody.[19]

1.3 On Feminism in Iran

Although impossible to date exactly, but there are records of people campaigning for women's rights from the mid-nineteenth century. For instance, Fatimah Baraghani/Umm-i-Salmih (1817–52), known as Táhirih or Qurrat al-Ayn, who was an influential poet and theologian, was the first woman to unveil in traditional Iran. Much later, Bibi Khanoom Astarabadi founded the first school for girls in Iran in 1907 (called simply The School for Girls) and wrote numerous articles in defence of the right of girls to receive universal education. Many female activists also took their veils off together and marched on the streets of Tehran in 1911, demanding the right to vote for women. Worth noting is also Taj al-Saltanah (1883–1936) who was the daughter of Naser al-Din Shah Qajar from the Qajar dynasty that ruled in Iran from 1785 to 1925. In her autobiographical work, al-Saltanah argues that postcolonial Iran could achieve its enlightenment goals of sovereignty, individual rights and technological progress only by discarding the traditional, oppressive practice of veiling and by promoting women's education.[20] She argued that covering was a sign of cultural backwardness and advocated full women's rights in the country.

Before the early twentieth century, in a male-dominated society, women were generally not educated in Iran and were confined to the home, rarely venturing outside. If a woman did need to go outside for a particular reason, she would have to cover herself from head to toe with a heavy veil. Thus, women were essentially prisoners in their own home or, in the case of concubines, the harem; at the very least, they were under the veil or cloak. As such, mothers had trained girls, to '[…] be humble, feeble, servile and dull. Therefore, the dominant feelings in their minds were self-disparagement, fear, and submissiveness'.[21]

There was no opportunity for women to socialize or gather, aside from rare occasions when they could meet in mosques, at baths or at times of religious mourning, or within their neighbourhoods in the small alleys between their houses. This situation continued until the 1906 Constitutional Revolution (1906–11). With representative government, educational reform and modernization chief among the objectives of the constitutionalists, this was a great time for women's awakening. Indeed, women's education was seen as a critical part of reforms that would pave the way for the creation and development of modern Iran.[22] A group of educated and enlightened women including Al-Saltaneh played a very strong role in this time of awakening in terms of the schools and societies they founded, the articles that they wrote and the journals they published. Combined, these significantly influenced the improvement of women's status in Iran.

After the Constitutional Revolution, many private schools for girls started to run classes. These schools were not supported by the government, but rather were run by a group of elite women who were educated in Europe and passionately wanted to increase literacy levels.[23] In such a traditional society, promoting women's education was not an easy task to take on, but despite all the setbacks the movement endured and around 30 years later, the government finally gave it official support (Act of Unveiling, 1936).

Following the 1936 Act of Unveiling, the Women's Association (Anjoman Banevan) in Iran was established and began to provide intensive support for women's education. The Women's Association was run by Sadighe Dowlatabadi, an important figure in the history of women's rights in Iran, who was born in 1882 in Isfahan.[24] As early as 1919, Dowlatabadi published the first women's periodical in Isfahan, called *Zaban-e Zanan* (*Women's Voice*), which immediately faced opposition from the mullahs in the city.[25] After closing the magazine down in Isfahan, Dowlatabadi moved to Tehran and, once again, started to publish it there. Copies of the magazine can be found in an archive collection at the International Institute of Social History (IISH) in Amsterdam, where I was able to consult them during my visits in July 2012, November 2014 and October 2015.

Women had begun to have more influence and presence in the world of journalism after the 1906–11 Constitutional Revolution, during which time women became more visible in society generally. According to Naomi Sakr, *Zaban-e Zanan* was, in fact, the third publication in Iran to focus on women's issues.[26] In 1918, Dr Kahal published a weekly magazine called *Danesh*, which ran for a year, during which only 30 issues were published. Another magazine, *Shekofeh*, was published by Mozin al-Saltaneh. In 1919, *Zaban-e Zanan* started to publish its four pages fortnightly. All the magazines were published by women who were the wives, daughters or sisters of male politicians, who could support and protect them in their endeavours. The aim was to make cultural and

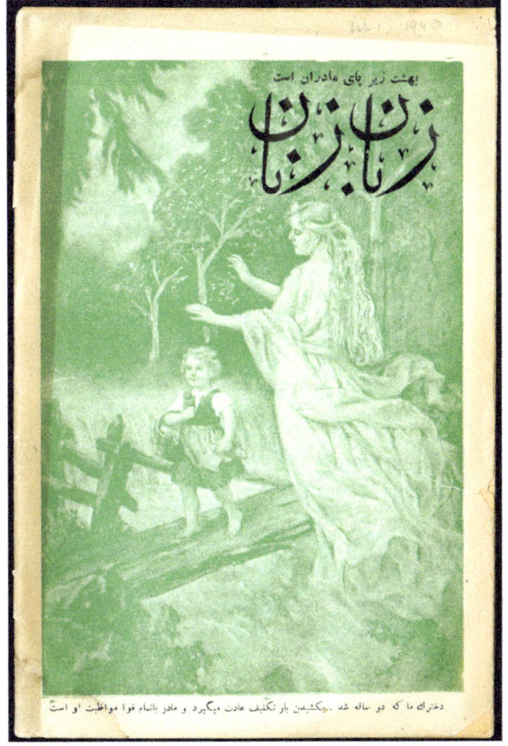

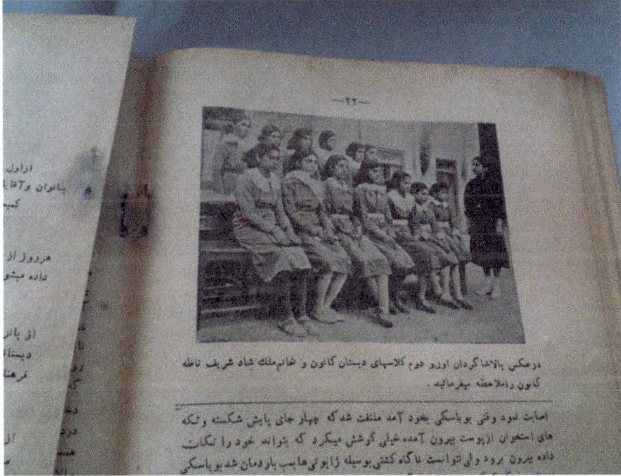

FIGURE 2: Sadighe Dowlatabadi documents and magazines. IISH Archive, Amsterdam. From top: a sample of Sadighe Dowlatabadi's handwriting, a cover of Women's Voice biweekly magazine; and a photo in a copy of *Women's Voice* with the caption (in Farsi) reading: 'The photo above is a group of students from level one and two in *Kanoon* school alongside Mrs Malak Shad Sharif Nazeh'.

educational material, both from a western and from a traditional perspective, accessible to Iranian women. From 1925 onwards, two other magazines were published, namely *Nameye Banevan, Dokhtarane Iran* and *Etelaate Banevan* (by Etelaat, one of the great publishing houses).

The work of women like Sadighe Dowlatabadi is certainly ground-breaking, and her life is one of the key moments in the history of women's rights in Iran. In 1947, Dowlatabadi participated in the 10th Congress of the International Woman Suffrage Alliance[27] in Paris, where she delivered a key speech about Iranian women. The congress board members were extremely pleased to welcome an Iranian representative for the first time. The International Woman Suffrage Alliance (IWSA) had emerged out of the International Council of Women (ICW) in 1902 and was formally established in 1904 in Berlin. The IWSA perceived itself as a representative of an international forum of women's movement activists for exchange, cooperation and coordination with a liberal feminist agenda. At the Paris congress in 1926, which was chaired by the Englishwoman Margery Corbett Ashby (1882–1981), the organization decided to rename itself the International Alliance of Women for Suffrage and Equal Citizenship.

Other key moments include the creation of the first official women's organization of Iran in 1966.[28] As a result of much hard work on the part of proponents of women's rights in Iran, many goals were eventually achieved, such as university education for women and the opening up of careers such as teaching and nursing. Even though this progress was an incredible feat and Iranian women entering the public domain and the workforce had previously been deemed unachievable, much work was still needed to increase women's rights. In light of this, the Women's Organisation of Iran (WOI) was established in 1966 to bring together all the small splinter groups that had formed within the women's movement. The intention was that everyone would fight for one common goal and achieve more in this way.

The WOI was a non-profit organization of 5000 members from diverse backgrounds and regions who, through consultation, brainstorming and negotiation, created a 50-member advisory group selected by the High Council of Iranian Women's Associations and its president, Princess Ashraf Pahlavi. The ultimate purpose and objectives of the WOI were as follows:

- To raise the cultural, social and economic knowledge of the women of Iran and to make them aware of their family, social and economic rights, duties and responsibilities (Article 1 of the Constitution).
- In order to realize its goals and its mission, the WOI shall undertake the following duties: defending the individual, family and social rights of women to ensure their complete equality in society and before the law (Article 2).[29]

The WOI ultimately had a life span of just over 12 years. During this period, it became one of the most vibrant and effective agents of change in terms of the status of women in the Global South.[30] This can be demonstrated by one of its major victories, namely the Family Protection Law of 1975, which granted women equal rights in marriage and divorce, enhanced their rights with regard to child custody, increased the minimum age of marriage to 18 for women and 20 for men and more or less eliminated polygamy. Abortion was also made legal, without arousing much public attention, by removing the penalty for performing the operation, which was previously found in medical malpractice laws. Further, labour laws and regulations were also revised to eliminate sexual discrimination and ensure equal pay for equal work. Women were also encouraged to run for political office.[31]

1.4 The Islamic Revolution of 1979

During the 1970s women gained a relatively strong position and status in society. The following statistics illustrate the fact that a large number of women were engaged in public life:

> The number of female candidates for universities had risen sevenfold during the first half of the 1970s. Women were scholars, police officers, judges, pilots and engineers. In 1978, 333 of the 1660 candidates for local councils were women. Twenty-two were elected to Parliament, two to the Senate. There was one female cabinet minister, one governor, one ambassador, five mayors.[32]

These figures clearly demonstrate that women were playing an active and visible role in Iranian society, but this all changed after the 1979 revolution when the compulsory dress code was announced.

The prime reason for the Iranian Revolution was the dissatisfaction with the Pahlavi monarchy that came to a head in 1979. The women's dress code played an important role in the symbolic politics of that time. In many images of the Revolution, women are seen wearing a *chador* when joining the mass street protest that occurred at that time. The vision of the Pahlavi monarch Reza Shah, which, as mentioned earlier, was implemented from 1925 onwards, was at that moment rejected through the introduction of the women's dress code. For Reza Shah, uncovering was a statement of his government's commitment to progress and development, so revolutionaries used the *chador* to turn against him.[33] So not all the women who wore a veil during the revolutionary protest did so for religious reasons; there was a mix of reasons among the group, as Katherine Bullock notes.[34] For some it was indeed a sign of religious identity, but for others it indicated nationalism or political populism among other things. Regardless of religious devotion, it is important to note that the one shared common goal and driving impetus behind all these veiled women was their commitment to the revolution.[35]

In the study that Katherine Bullock undertook in Muslim countries, she describes seven major motivations for women's covering, i.e. revolutionary protest, political protest, religious, continued access to the public sphere, statement of personal identity, custom and state law. She adds that there is of course some overlap between these, and that, depending on the Muslim country concerned, there may well be a number of these motivations actively present at the same time that results in the veiled woman's body. Bullock notes that the images of Iranian and Afghani women are the most represented images when it comes to the notion of state law forced covering, and that in Algeria and some other Muslim countries women cover due to the threat of physical violence.[36]

The Islamic Revolution in Iran (1979) began with Supreme Leader Ruhollah Khomeini (Ayatollah Khomeini) calling for the foundation of an Islamic state based on Islamic principles and the upholding of Islamic law. It imposed the veiling of women[37] as a visible symbol of that commitment. The way in which Ayatollah Khomeini's views formed the basis of Iranian legislation and policies was similar to the way in which Reza Shah had established his vision at the start of the Pahlavi dynasty. For instance, to protect the Islamic Republic and guarantee its survival, Ayatollah Khomeini established a public space governed by Islamic principles and values, essentially meaning the segregation of genders and the veiling of women.[38] Naturally, there is some overlap between these and more than one of these motivations may apply in the same country and to the same woman.[39]

As noted above, 'to cover' or 'to veil' are the equivalent of the Farsi words *'poshesh'* or *'hijab'*, meaning that the hair and body of women should be concealed by fabric. The understanding of the specific requirements of the *hijab* – for example, whether it should extend to covering the hands and face – has been, and continues to be, a point of argument among legal traditions and individual jurists. In post-revolutionary Iran, coverings took two forms; the first was the full veil that stretched from head to toe and the second was a headscarf accompanied by a loose long-sleeved garment. In reality, mixed forms could also often be seen.

The enforcement of the dress code after the 1979 revolution stems from the radical attitude of Islamic fundamentalism towards women and the covering of the body. Islamic fundamentalists[40] believe that women should cover themselves in order to prevent sexual tension in society because men are not capable of controlling their sexual desire.[41] In Muslim families, girls are considered adults from the age of nine. Thus, after a formal ceremony in the mosque called a *task (Jashn-e Taklif)*, they need to start covering their body and hair by wearing the veil and/or a long tunic and loose pair of trousers whenever they are in public or in the presence of men who are not family members or relatives.

The enforcement of the Islamic dress code in Iran is based on the teachings of the Quran, which includes injunctions such as 'women must lower their gaze[42] and guard their private parts and not expose their adornment in public'.[43] Ayatollah Khomeini recited the Quran himself, saying '*woman is a pearl* that is best hidden in an *oyster* shell'[44] and explained that the covering was designed to protect women from being sexually objectified when out in public. This Islamic belief emerged in medieval legal scholarship that focuses on women's modest dress as a way to prevent *fitna* or worldly disorder.[45] Elizabeth Bucar calls this a form of public chastity, observing that 'men and women can interact in public but only in ways that avoid any sexual impropriety'.[46] Therefore, women are required to cover themselves in order to reduce sexual tension in society. For many Islamic scholars like Mortaza Mottahari, the dress code is a mechanism through which the ideal public chastity can be created and maintained.[47] However, it is not always clear who should be or who needs to be protected from whom, and there seems to be a constant and yet undelineated negotiation going on between men and women who are perpetually in the dangerous position of invading each other's boundaries.[48]

> *As I pulled the chador over me,*
> *I felt a heaviness descending over me.*
> *I was hidden and hiding.*
> *There was nothing visible left from Sousan Azadi....*
> *I was just another faceless Muslim woman carrying a whole inner world*
> *hidden inside the chador.*
>
> Sousan Azadi[49]

After the revolution, women could not 'wear obvious colours, make-up, perfume, or anything that might attract the attention of the *Basij* or "moral police"' (for more please see page 73).[50] 'Black from head to toe' is an expression that is commonly used to describe the woman's body covered in the full veil, but in reality this is not the case. In fact, women could wear a long loose garment and long headscarf as long as it was a dark colour such as dark blue, black and grey. The expression thus more accurately refers to the idea of fundamentalist (Islamists) encouraging women to wear dark colours rather than referring solely to the full veil.

With the passage of time, some of the rights that women had gained under the Shah (such as the Family Protection Law and equal rights in marriage and divorce) were systematically taken away by legislation and laws such as the compulsory *hijab* were introduced. Suddenly, women were restricted and repressed, essentially deprived of their basic liberties. The Iranian Revolution was designed to achieve greater independence and freedom for the people, but what happened for women was, in fact, the opposite.

The day after the announcement of the compulsory dress code, men and women spontaneously marched on the streets of Tehran in opposition to the decision. The demonstration continued for six days. During the first few days, women were using just small pieces of paper to write their fairly rudimentary slogans on, but by days four and five, they were using curtains and marker pens and being far more effective. At the time of these protests, the American feminist author Kate Millett was in Iran, attending a conference at Tehran University for International Women's Day, which also fell on 8 March. She stated that she was extremely impressed by the Women's Uprising, noting in an interview[51] that in America, a demonstration of this scale would require many years of planning and writing to women to try and persuade them to take part. On this occasion, in stark contrast, she was surprised that a thousand or so people had, seemingly overnight, simply taken it upon themselves to meet at a particular location. This had never happened before in the history of feminism.

Many journalists arrived in Iran on the third day of demonstrations to capture this momentous event. An interesting documentary film entitled *Mouvement de Libération des Femmes Iraniennes: Année Zéro Pratique* made by four French journalists from the group Politique et Psychanalyse[52] – Michelle Muller, Sylvina Boissonnas, Claudine Mulard and Sylviane Rey – part of the Mouvement de Libération des Femmes, recorded the event. In the course of this video, journalists are seen and heard asking participants the reason that they were out on the streets. One woman responds passionately: 'We are here for freedom. We are as many men as women. With or without the veil, we fight for freedom, for us and for the people'. The woman talks expressively about her desire for freedom, even if the price is to forego one's religion; she prefers to be free and not be under the control of an enforced religion. An old woman in a patterned veil explains:

> I have been wearing the chador for years now for my own personal reasons. I'm not here to try to stop wearing the chador; rather I'm the mother of six daughters and I am protesting because I don't want them to be forced to wear the chador if they don't want to. I'm here to defend my daughters from the enforcement of the chador by men.

In the video, another young woman who is a student at Tehran University talks about feeling entrapped: 'We are protesting for our rights on equality and freedom', she explains vehemently, adding that

> we need to protest now and voice our demands before the constitution is written. Otherwise, they will not make any allowances for women after the law has

been passed. We are not protesting against the veil only, but for all these other issues connected to forcibly veiling someone, which we believe are much more important than just the act of veiling itself.

The student adds that, '[t]he lawyers were the first to protest. We supported the revolution on certain goals, which is why we joined them, but now they have a different opinion'.

The objective of the six days of protest in Iran was not only to reject the compulsory dress code but to highlight the initial purpose of the revolution, i.e. to secure greater freedom and equality for the people. The protesters were fighting for equal pay for men and women, and for freedom of the press, speech and assembly. The aim of this remarkable spontaneous protest, the first of its kind in the feminist history of Iran, was to protect the rights and autonomy of women away from the authority of the men who sought to force them to cover.

In 2015 at the Comité des Femmes Contre la Lapidation in France, as part of the 8th March International Women's Day celebrations, Shahin Nawai[53] presented her fascinating account of the demonstration on the same date in 1979. Nawai is one of the executive committee members of the council (*showra*) that created the National Unity of Women's Associations during the 1979 uprising. She was educated in California, and after her return to Iran, worked at the University of Tehran. On 8 March 1979, Nawai and her friends decided to support the women's movement in order to try and stop women's rights being taken away from them in the process of the Islamization of society. They believed they were protecting the future of all women in Iran, and were joined by feminists from France, Germany, Egypt and many other countries, all of whom were anxious to lend their support to Iranian women. This led to the creation of a Solidarity Committee (CIDF), which was led by Simone de Beauvoir (Figure 3). Nawai notes that the uprising became calmer on the fourth day when Mahmoud Taleghani from the government came to talk to the people and tried to persuade them that Khomeini was not, in fact, enforcing the wearing of the *hijab*, but was rather suggesting that women should be encouraged to wear it for the purposes of public order and decency.

Unfortunately, these statements did not prove to be true, and over time, it did, in fact, become compulsory for all women in Iran to cover themselves. It began in hospitals and offices where employers started to fire women who were not willing to cover themselves. In Masjed Soleyman (Figure 4) (a city in south-west Iran), for instance, 40 female nurses were all let go on the same day (8 March 1979) because they would not accept the covering as part of their uniform. Many doctors were actually against this for hygiene reasons, claiming that the long loose clothing made it easier to spread dirt and bacteria, but these warnings were not heeded.

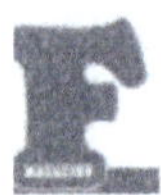

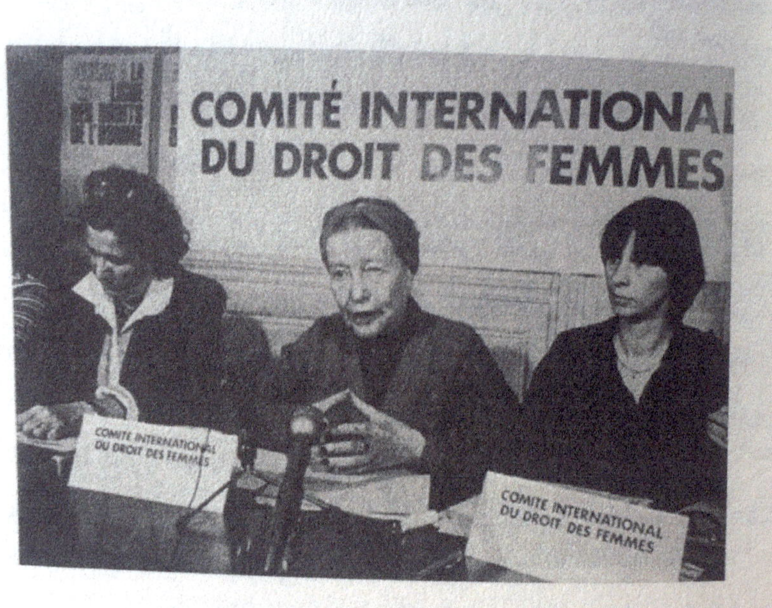

سیمون دوبووآر، ماریا آنتونی‌یتا ماسیوچی (سمت چپ) و الیزابت سالوارزی(سمت راست)،
پنجشنبه ۱۵ مارس:جلسه‌ی اعلام موجودیت C.I.D.F.

FIGURE 3: The creation of a Solidarity Committee (CIDF), which was led by Simone de Beauvoir, 1979, Paris.

At the same time, there were many other changes to women's lives in Iran, several of which are detailed below. Most notably, sweeping reforms to family law saw the legal age for marriage for girls lowered from 18 to just 9; such a reform was perceived as opening the way to legalized child abuse. The number of women in the workplace also fell dramatically within three years. Between 1979 and 1981, women were checked at the gates of their workplace to make sure they were properly veiled and not wearing make-up. A de facto gender apartheid segregating men and women was established in the streets, extending to the workplace, public transport, cinemas, queues and so on. Film and TV were heavily censored, with unveiled female actresses having to be blacked out. The morality police could forcefully break into private parties at any time to check who was present and what was going on, and no socialization was allowed between unrelated men and women. Primitive laws, including flogging and stoning, were also passed, in response to the re-actualization of the concept of 'an eye for an eye'. National Women's Day was set as 12 June, the birthday of Fatimah, the daughter of the Prophet Muhammad. Gradually, the Islamic government also started to demolish cultural centres (*marakeze refahe khanevade*). The first to be demolished were the local cultural centres, which were civic buildings where women would meet to learn about childcare, housework and other pursuits. Due to the disappearance of these places, Nawai and the National Unity of Women's Associations decided to run private sessions in Tehran and beyond, to keep trying to educate women and pass on the most up-to-date information available, away from the control and interference of the Islamists. Nawai says she deeply regretted the way the government and media reacted to the uprising. The women were accused of supporting the Pahlavi dynasty that had been overthrown, and in engaging in an act of prostitution. The government would not negotiate and the movement was largely ignored.

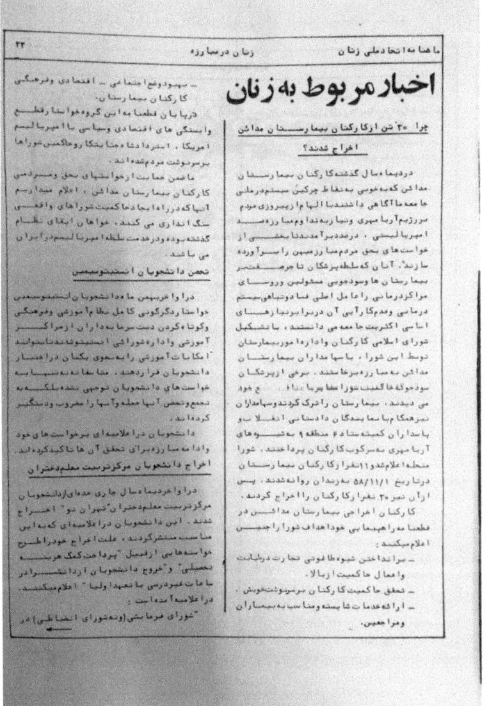

اخبار مربوط به زنان

چرا ۴۰ تن از کارکنان بیمارستان مداین اخراج شدند؟

FIGURE 4: *Mahnameh Etehad Meli Zanan* (*Monthly Magazine of the National Unity of Women*) (1979). Archiv fur Forschung und Dokumentation Iran – Berlin (AFDI), Berlin. It reads: 'in Masjed Soleyman 40 female nurses were all let go on the same day (8 March 1979) because they would not accept the covering as part of their uniform'.

Since 8 March 1979 there have been other such demonstrations. In 2009 people marched through the streets of Tehran to protest against the repressive regime. 2009 – the 30th anniversary of the original 1979 protest – saw a huge uprising of students and other young people in response to the contested presidential election that occurred in that year. It was at that moment that I saw the extent of the power of revolt. Even though the uprising of 2009 did not achieve any *real* progress, it was a remarkable moment where men and women once again stood together to jointly voice their dissatisfaction with the regime. The solidarity of the crowd was indisputable, and took the government by surprise; they were shocked by the size of the demonstration, and as such used any means at their disposal to try to stop the uprising.

Inspired by the 30th anniversary of the uprising in 2009, Nasser Mohajer and Mahnaz Matin decided to compile a comprehensive record of the original 1979 event. In doing so, they researched the vast amount of newspaper and magazine material, and also conducted a series of interviews with women who were there. All the material collected resulted in the creation of an archive and two-volume publication in the Farsi language entitled *The Post-Revolutionary Women's Uprising of March 1979* (Khizesh Zanan dar Esfande 1357, Tavalodi Digar).[54] In an interview conducted with the authors by Dr Eskandar Sadeghi-Boroujerdi, Matin notes that,

> The March 8, 1979 uprising was the first protest movement to emerge following the revolution from within the revolution itself and against the actions of the leadership. Such an event was unprecedented and it was for this reason that it attracted the attention of feminists around the world.[55]

It seems that ever since that historical demonstration, and the recent events of 2009, there has been an ongoing feminist revolt or civil society action in what is essentially a totalitarian state of Iran.

At this juncture, it is important to draw attention to *The Origins of Totalitarianism* by Hannah Arendt,[56] a work that looks at Nazi Germany. With its total theocratic control of all aspects of individual existence, Khomeini's state had much more in common with Hannah Arendt's description of Hitler's state. The Islamic Republic did not leave any area of life – political, social, private, public or otherwise – to the discretion of its citizens. It was the 1960s where Islam really started to become a powerful force in Iranian politics. During the 1960s, Shi'ite fundamentalists started to become more active, encouraging students to stand up and fight against the modernization of society (and, in turn, against the Pahlavi monarchy). This movement was started by Ayatollahs Najafabadi and Khomeini. Their aim was to halt modernization and establish an Islamic idealist culture (Islamic utopia).

Eventually, the Islamic Shi'ite fundamentalist movement succeeded in initiating the 1979 revolution, and they have governed the country ever since. There was a short break of eight years during Mohammad Khatami's reformist presidency (1997–2005), but apart from this fairly brief period, since 1979, Iran has been ruled by Islamic fundamentalist Shi'ism. While Reza Shah and his son had established a dictatorship prior to the dominance of Islam, totalitarianism was at the heart of the Islamic Republic, as in Nazi Germany.

One hypothesis is that the Islamic Republic's humiliation and suppression of women in Iran is a policy designed to control society as a whole. As such, the Iranian women's movement should be viewed as a form of civil resistance, with implications far beyond the national boundaries of Iran itself. If this holds, the Iranian women's movement is thus an anti-totalitarian movement. Upon close examination, it appears that the focus of the feminist movement in Iran has always been about reclaiming human dignity for all people. While Swedish and Dutch feminists, for instance, ask for more and better childcare facilities for their children so that they can go out to work, and for more leadership positions for women in industry, Iranian feminists, in contrast, are still struggling to achieve basic human rights in their own country.[57] It is instructive to note that women were the first to notice the totalitarian threat of the Islamic government, a fact that was expressed clearly and unambiguously on 8 March 1979. As already noted, the emphasis of the feminist movement in Iran is on human dignity, and opposition to totalitarianism. Such a movement transcends cultural and gender boundaries, which is why both men and women, and people from other countries and cultures, were so keen to become involved and show their support.

By April 1983, the compulsory veil was in full force, applying to all women in Iran regardless of their nationality. The National Unity of Women's Associations was dismantled by the government, and Nawai and her team emigrated to cities such as London and Berlin. As Nawai argues, feminism and Islam are unable to exist in harmony because Islam does not really provide for equality, open discussion and individual choice or prerogative, which by its nature is the core of feminism.[58]

The new veil worn following the revolution soon came to represent the 'state' and was no longer simply an expression of religious belief; as such, it was seen in a different way to the traditional covering. Before 1979, women who had worn a veil had done so because of their own personal belief; it had been entirely a matter of personal choice. It should be noted that at that time what women could or could not wear was a matter of tradition and was not stipulated by law. Women, therefore, had some degree of choice so long as they respected certain broad conventions; for instance, with regard to what type of clothing was deemed suitable for their social class. However, after the revolution, women who had previously chosen not to wear the veil were suddenly branded 'infidels' or 'bad hijab'.[59]

Veiling soon became indissociable from the wider Muslim identity and the veiled Iranian woman's own religious belief became subsumed to her status as an Islamic icon. As mentioned above, Katherine Bullock cites this as one of the seven motivations she has identified for women veiling, referring to 'revolutionary protest' as the most dramatic re-covering phenomenon of the twentieth century. Bullock provides the examples of the anti-colonial and revolutionary struggles in Algeria during the 1950s and Iran during the 1970s. In both cases, women were not covered before the protests, but donned the veil/*chador* to help overthrow the oppressive government of the time.[60]

1.5 On Photography

I would like to end where I began, with the photograph and its particular place in Iranian history. The history of photography in Iran is different from other Middle Eastern societies because of how it was introduced solely to the court, as a royal practice, and that it has specifically been developed through this channel. It was not until the 1880s that photography finally found its way outside of the four walls of the palace, and the first commercial studio outside the court was established by Antoin Sevrogin.

The camera was introduced into Iran in 1842, during the reign of Nasir al-Din Shah Qajar (reigned 1848–96). The King had become fascinated with the new technology during a visit to Europe, and requested that a daguerreotype camera to be sent to his court. The camera was sent from Moscow.[61] Later, in 1848, the crown prince, Nasir al-Din Shah Qajar hired French tutor/photographer Francis Carlihan to teach photography at court. At the end of the same year, the Royal Photography Atelier (*akkas khane-ye mobarake-ye homayuni*) was established in the grounds of Golestan Palace. This was the moment when the Shah started to receive photography lessons from Carlihan primarily so that he could take pictures of the women of harems and his children. Shah also appointed Aqa Riza Iqbal al-Saltana, one of his favourite court members, to receive photographic lessons during the same time. The practice of photography in Iran thus started as an exclusively royal practice, and only the King took pictures of women.[62]

It is important to note that the representation of the Middle East began from the visual documentation of European travellers and indigenous artists. The photograph, as Ali Behdad notes, was used as an 'illustrative and constitutive notion of the Orient in the form of either a state archive, tourist album, magazine cover or picture postcard'.[63] During the Qajar and Ottoman dynasties, during which time photography was introduced to the Middle East, the medium was used not only as a means of reproduction and mass production to foreground the social status and dynastic power of the royal family, but also to represent the region's historical monuments and diverse population.

'Photo-exoticism', the ethnographic representation of indigenous people, which is the major theme of orientalist photography, was not widely seen in Iran. The reason for this was the cultural and religious restrictions in Persian society during that era. For instance, the women of the harem, which provides some of the most exotic photography in North Africa and the Near East, are not represented in Iran. The harem in Iran was photographed only by Naser al-Din Shah Qajar, and these photographs were kept in the King's personal collection (*albom khaneh*) in Golestan Palace. During this era, men were not permitted to visit Persian harems, and in contrast to other Middle Eastern lands, European visitors were not able to capture women in the harem setting. In this regard, the only remaining document by visitors that provides representation of the Persian women of the harem is writing, in particular, *fiction*.

Thus, the history of photography in Iran can be divided into four phases.

- The first phase, characterized as 'The Early Years of the Daguerreotype' (1842–52), saw the camera being introduced into Persia. Unfortunately, there are no daguerreotypes held by museums in Iran.[64]
- The second phase was 'The Formative Years' (1850–80), in which two events deeply affected the development of photography: first, the coronation of a young, enthusiastic king who was fascinated by photography; and second the establishment of Iran's first modern technical college, Dar al-Funun, on the grounds of the King's palace, where photography and chemistry featured as part of the curriculum, salt-print and wet-collodion techniques were taught and practised there, and court photographers were trained under the title of 'Akasbashi', and sent on photographic expeditions around the country. This was the time that photographic practice really took root among the royal family and other affluent people. Some 43,000 images and 1000 albums are the result of Naser al-Din Shah Qajar's historical photographic production, reflecting the fashion, architecture, urban development and socio-economic conditions in Iran during this era.
- The third period, 1880–1900, were 'The Years of Transition' (1880–1900), which saw the camera finally leaving the confines of the palace and entering public life. It was at this point that photographic studios were established in most major cities.
- Finally, there was the 'Turmoil and Photo-Documentation' (1900–25) phase, during which time studio photographers significantly expanded their business. Photo-documentation became more popular during this time. Since the following two decades marked a period of great political disturbance, during

which time the Constitutional Revolution took place (1906–11), resulting in many unstable sociopolitical conditions, the camera was able to play a highly effective role within the public visual space. Images of the protagonists were framed in photographs, and built, celebrated and defamed by words in vociferous journals and pamphlets. This was perhaps the beginning of reportage photography in Iran.

At the same time, photographic portraiture became more widespread, and faces captured on dry collodion glass plates and printed in albumen formed the nucleus of the modern Iranian middle class. Under conditions of extreme volatility and increased momentum of sociopolitical change, photography was used to create a collective memory through the accumulation of an image bank. Art photography was still yet to be born at this point.

The representation of women in the history of Iranian photography has been limited by cultural and religious restrictions as well as by the fact that photography

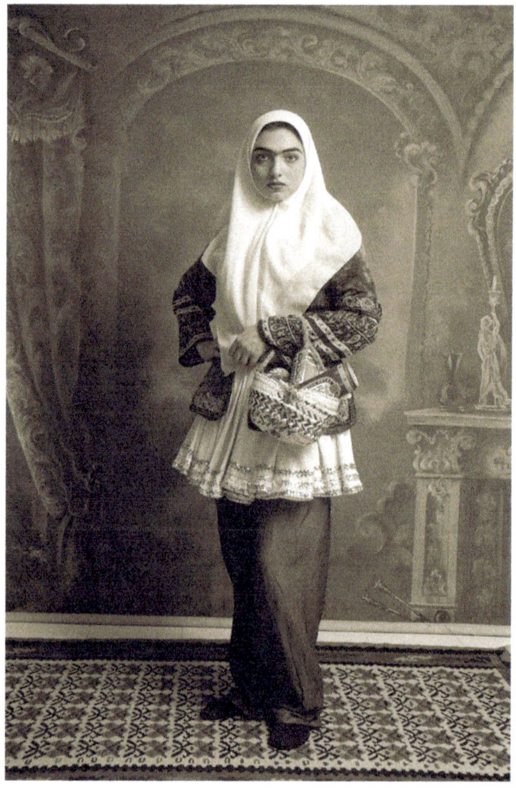

FIGURE 5: Shadi Ghadirian, Qajar series (1998). Photograph. Tehran.

was, for some time, the exclusive domain of the King. The kind of nude images of women that have come out of North Africa have never really been seen in Iranian photography; the photographs that emerged during the Qajar period were mainly portraiture.[65] There are images of women of the harem, wearing sheer blouses or displaying bare legs under their skirt, but these were only taken by Naser al-Din Shah Qajar.

In sepia-toned images that are part of the Qajar series (1998), Shadi Ghadirian has restaged the fashion of female clothing during the Persian Qajar dynasty alongside a series of coded props, such as a can of Coca Cola, a bicycle, a vacuum cleaner, a padded jacket with 'USA' inscribed on the back and a ghetto blaster.[66] In the full-length portraits, the full-face view orientation emphasizes the gaze of the figure looking straight at the camera (Figure 8). Although there are other photographs in the Qajar series that show figures wearing the full niqab, the impression remains that the figure is looking directly (defiantly) at the camera (that is, the viewer). Women are, in this way, given a gaze upon us, upon the world. Furthermore, Ghadirian's portraits evoke tradition through the use of not only antiquated backdrops and costumes, but also the position of women between the idea of tradition and western modernism (cultural, technological, consumerist).

Here, the photographer is a woman (Ghadirian) claiming in the present a position that would have been denied to her under Naser al-Din Shah Qajar's reign. This powerful restaging by a woman photographer of the problematic position of the Iranian woman between stifling tradition and sterile western consumerism, I believe, claims the democratic presence of women in Iranian photography. Whereas, in Gohari photographs the gaze of the woman is denied and the body is hidden under layers of fabric, here, in Ghadirian's work, the female gaze upon the looker is clear, steady and critical.

NOTES

9.   Elizabeth Bucar, *Pious Fashion: How Muslim Women Dress* (Cambridge: Harvard University Press, 2017), 26–27.

10.   Badr ol-Moluk Bamdad and Nasin Rahimieh, *From Darkness into Light: Women's Emancipation in Iran* (Costa Mesa: Mazda Publishers, 1980), 7–23.

11.   This speech more or less echoed what Taj al-Saltanah had said in 1906. See Abbas Amanat (ed.), *Taj Al-Saltana: Crowning Anguish: Memories of a Persian Princess from the Harem to Modernity 1884–1914*, trans. Anna Vanzan and Amin Neshati (Washington, DC: Mage Publishers, 2003), 200.

12.   Bamdad and Rahimieh, *From Darkness into Light*, 7–23.

13.   Bucar, *Pious Fashion*, 25.

14.   Ibid., 26–27.

15. Bamdad and Rahimieh, *From Darkness into Light*, 7–23.

16. Bucar, *Pious Fashion*, 27.

17. Nima Naghibi, *Rethinking Global Sisterhood: Western Feminism and Iran* (Minneapolis: University of Minnesota Press, 2007), 51.

18. Haideh Daragahi and Nina Witoszek, 'Anti-Totalitarian Feminism? Civic Resistance in Iran', in *Civil Society in the Age of Monitory Democracy*, Studies on Civil Society, ed. Lars Trägardh, Nina Witoszek and Bron Taylor (Oxford: Berghahn Books, 2013), 231–54.

19. Daragahi and Witoszek, 'Anti-Totalitarian Feminism?', 244.

20. Amanat, *Taj Al-Saltana: Crowning Anguish*, 200.

21. Bamdad and Rahimieh, *From Darkness into Light*, 18.

22. Ibid., viii.

23. Daragahi and Witoszek, 'Anti-Totalitarian Feminism?', 231–54.

24. Homeira Ranjbar Omrani, *Jameyat zanan* (*Women Association of Iran*) (Tehran: Nazar Print, 2004), 59.

25. About 30 years earlier than Dowlatabadi, it was Hind Nawfal (1860–1920) who established the first women's magazine in the Arab world. The Arabic press in Egypt was flourishing by the 1880s and included a number of monthlies as well as other magazines that appeared less regularly. Some journals like *Al-Muqtataf* (founded at the Syrian Protestant College, now the American University of Beirut) were devoted mostly to science. Others like *Al-Hilal* (founded in Egypt by a journalist from Beirut) discussed literature. On 20 November 1892 the first Arabic monthly designed specifically for women appeared in Alexandria. Called *Al-Fatah* ('The Young Girl') it was owned and edited by a woman, namely Hind Nawfal. See Margot Badran and Miriam Cooke, *Opening the Gates: A Century of Arab Feminist Writing* (London: Virago, 1990), 251.

26. Gholam Khiabany and Annabele Sreberny, 'The Women's Press in Contemporary Iran: Engendering the Public Sphere', in *Women and Media in the Middle East: Power Through Self-Expression*, ed. Naomi Sakr (London: I.B. Tauris, 2004), 18.

27. Jasmin Khosravi, *Zabān-i Zanān – The Voice of Women: The Life and Work of Ṣadīqa Daulatābādī (1882–1961)* (Berlin: Eb-Verlag, 2012). Extract in English from original German.

28. Khiabany and Sreberny, 'The Women's Press in Contemporary Iran', 18.

29. 'About Women's Organisation of Iran', Women's Organisation of Iran, last modified 20 April 2014, http://fis-iran.org/en/women/organization.

30. Ibid.

31. 'Introduction to Women's Organisation of Iran', Women's Organisation of Iran, last modified 20 April 2014, http://fisiran.org/en/women/organization/introduction.

32. Ali Razi, *Tarih-I-Mofassal-I-Iran* (*The Complete History of Iran*) (Tehran: Eghbal and Shorakae Publication, 1956), 661.

33. Katherine Bullock, *Rethinking Muslim Women and the Veil: Challenging Historical and Modern Stereotypes* (Herndon: International Institute of Islamic Thought, 2007), 89.

34. Ibid., 90.

35. Ibid., 94.

36. Ibid., 94.

37. Ibid., 95–96.

38. Ibid., 98.

39. Ibid., 104.

40. Please note that some scholarly works refer to Islamic fundamentalists as Islamists or Political Islamists.

41. Morteza Motahhari, *The Problem of Hijab* (Tehran: Basir Publication, 1986), 29.

42. A similar instruction is also given to men in the previous verse.

43. 'Islamic Rules of Modesty for Women', Quran Surat al-Nur Verse 31, last modified 28 September 2015, http://quran.com/24/31.

44. 'Hidden Pearls', Islam Great Religion, last modified 4 December 2010, https://islamgreatreligion/wordpress.com/2010/12/04/hidden-pearls/.

45. Bucar, *Pious Fashion*, 56.

46. Ibid., 58.

47. Ibid., 59.

48. Even though the scope of the book is Iranian society, it is important to note that perhaps outside Iran sexual harassment policies for the workplace aim to define similar issues about boundaries.

49. Farzaneh Milani, *Veils and Words: The Emerging Voices of Iranian Women Writers* (New York: Syracuse University Press, 1992), 44.

50. Masserat Amir-Ebrahimi, 'Transgression in Narration: The Lives of Iranian Women in Cyberspace', in 'Innovative Women: Unsung Pioneers of Social Change', special issue, *Journal of Middle East Women's Studies* 4, no. 3 (Fall 2008): 80–118.

51. Pratique, Politique et Psychanalyse (Michele Moulder, Sylvia Boiasuna, Claudine Mular and Sylven Rey), *Mouvement de Libération des Femmes Iraniennes: Année Zero*, France, 1979, YouTube, last modified 20 April 2015, https://www.youtube.com/watch?v=ulJwXHji6f4.

52. Ibid.

53. Shahin Nawai, 'Le Comité des Femmes Contre la Lapidation, Paris', presentation, last accessed 6 April 2014, https://www.youtube.com/watch?v=_7mnB_exy9I.

54. Mahnaz Matin and Naser Mohajer, *Iranian Women's Uprising March 8th 1979 Vol. I: Renaissance,* Cologne: Nuqṭa Publishing, 2010.

55. 'The Post-Revolutionary Women's Uprising of March 1979: An Interview with Nasser Mohajer and Mahnaz Matin', Iran Wire, last accessed 12 October 2015, http://en.iran-wire.com/features/944/.

56. Hannah Arendt, *On Revolution* (London: Penguin Books, 1963), 65–68.

57. Daragahi and Witoszek, 'Anti-Totalitarian Feminism?', 231–54.

58. Nawai, 'Le Comité des Femmes'.

59. Amir-Ebrahimi, 'Transgression in Narration', 92.

60. Bullock, *Rethinking Muslim Women and the Veil*, 87.

61. 'History of Photography in Iran', The Freer|Sackler, last accessed 20 April 2014, https://www.asia.si.edu/iran-in-photographs/intro-photography.asp

62. For this brief history of the origin of Iranian photography I am indebted to: Khadijeh Mohammadi Nameghi and Carmen Perez Gonzalez, 'From Sitters to Photographers: Women in Photography from the Qajar Era to the 1930s', in *History of Photography: The First Hundred Years of Iranian Photography* (London: Routledge, 2013, vol. 37, no. 1), 87–110.

63. Ali Behdad, 'The Orientalist Photograph', in *Photography's Orientalism: New Essays on Colonial Representation*, eds. Ali Behdad and Luke Gartlan (Los Angeles, CA: Getty Publications, 2013), 33–46.

64. There are some available at Freer Sackler, The Smithsonian's Museum of Asian Art, Washington, DC.

65. Ali Behdad, 'The Orientalist Photograph', 95.

66. Harriet Riches, 'Shadow Sites', *Afterimage* 40, no. 6 (May/June 2013): 32.

Chapter Two

2.1 On Veiling and Writing

Across Iranian history, the women's movement has gone through two major processes of change: in terms of its activity in the public domain, and in terms of its access to self-expression through writing.[67] Writing, with its great potential for public communication and entering the world of others, could be considered no less a transgression than unveiling. Through both, a woman can express – and expose – herself publicly. Through both, an absence becomes a presence. Both are powerful means of expression and communication, while the one gives the woman's voice a body, the other gives her body a voice. On this point, it can be seen that even though the act of unveiling that occurred in 1936 brought women out of the home and into the public domain (more or less), it took almost 30 years for the first work of fiction by a woman writer to be published in 1969. In fact, the physical act of unveiling (1936) had a significant impact, both positive and negative, on all social classes. For the majority of women, in particular the middle classes, came the opportunity to start a new life outside the home, to discover a whole new world beyond their front door. This led to increased levels of education amongst women, and women being able to become more active members of society. It was at this point that both fiction and non-fiction became accepted forms of literary expression for women (1970s).

Simin Daneshvar's *Savushun*[68] was the first work of fiction written by a female author to be published in Iran (in 1969). Prior to this, Daneshvar had been a key figure in unfolding female Persian literature in Iran. *Suvashun* was published during a period of political and economic upheaval, when oil was nationalized and the Mohammad Mossadegh coup caused real economic hardship. Daneshvar's aim, through fiction and storytelling, is to bring together the implication of writing as a form of narrative that maps the social and political transformation of a society (in this case, Iran). 'Savushun', as in the title of the novel, *Mourners of Siyavash*, also known as *A Persian Requiem,* refers to a folk tradition surviving in southern Iran from an unknown pre-Islamic time. It conjures up hope; in spite of everything, it suggests the transformation of hopelessness into salvation. This idea is evoked in some detail in the final pages using a metaphor of the flame of idealism against the backdrop of hopelessness and helplessness, a notion found in many traditions, both religious and secular. It is a unique piece of literature, which is able to transcend the boundaries of the historical community in which it was written.

The narrative develops using the basic paradigms of Iranian womanhood and married life. The centrality of the life of the family and of Zari (the protagonist in the story) is a major factor that contributes to the book's appeal. Using the household as a stage, the author weaves a narrative of steadily increasing complexity, involving a variety of situations and personalities that work through the gamut of Iranian collective concerns. The household includes Zari's maturing son, her twin daughters, her widow sister-in-law and various devoted servants. Her principled husband spends extended periods of time away in the village. Frequent visitors to the household include Zari's ambitious brother-in-law and headstrong tribal leader who are rebelling against the government. The theatrical choir in the background expresses a variety of social, political and economic concerns within the family circle.

The story is set in the mid-twentieth century (1941–45), a period when Iran was reduced to its most abject state of dependence in its modern history, while still nominally retaining its own independent government under the young shah, Mohammad Reza Shah. Poverty was widespread, and disease rates were high, with typhus, in particular, a chronic problem. Corruption, incompetence and arrogance were the characteristics of the vast majority of people in authority, whether national or local government, the army or the police. The author's choice of location in and around Shiraz during the Second World War is apposite, in that the interplay between Islamic and pre-Islamic ideas and rituals is one of the most significant strand in the book. The setting evokes images of shrines and Sufis (practitioners of a mystical dimension of Islam), of the great monuments and tombs dating back to pre-Islamic Iran and, in the hinterland, of the nomadic tribes.

Indeed, thinking about the domestic setting of *Savushun* reminds me of Forough Farrokhzad's theatrical poem called 'Delam Barae Baghche Misozad' ('I Feel Sorry for the Garden') (1958),[69] which is beautifully centred in a family setting and expresses a collective vision of different generations of father/mother and brother/sister towards the prevailing social concerns. It was written by arguably the most famous woman in the history of Persian literature, Farrokhzad (1935–67) who was a poet of great audacity and extraordinary talent. Her poetry was the poetry of protest, of protest through revelation – revelation in the sense of the innermost world of women (a taboo subject until then), their intimate secrets and desires, their sorrows, longings, aspirations and, at times, even the voicing of their feelings in silence. Farrokhzad's expressions of physical and emotional intimacy, much lacking in Persian women's poetry up to that point, placed her at the centre of controversies, even among other intellectuals of the time.

> *My sister was a friend to flowers.*
> *She would take her simple heart's words*
> *– when Mother beat her –*
> *to their kind and silent gathering*
> *and sometimes she would treat the family*
> *of fish to sunshine and cake crumbs.*
> *She now lives on the other side of town*
> *in her artificial home*
> *and in the arms of her artificial husband*
> *she makes natural children.*
> *Each time she visits us, if her skirt is sullied*
> *with the poverty of our garden*
> *she bathes herself in perfume.*
> *Every time she visits she is with child.*
> *Our garden is forlorn*
> *Our garden is forlorn.*[70]

In Farrokhzad's early poems, the garden is a locus characterized by hope and life, a setting shielded from much of the negativity that surrounds the speaker. However, the most profound/positive description of the garden by Farrokhzad is in her poem 'I Feel Sorry for the Garden', published in 1974. In contrast to her earlier poems, the garden is presented as a source of negativity, characterized by putridity, death and suppressed feelings of anger and frustration. The garden depicted in 'I Feel Sorry for the Garden' is located in an urban setting in a family home and is the heart or nucleus of the family's life itself. The garden is a *'baghche'* or *'hayat'*, the small courtyard garden typically found at the centre of traditional Iranian homes, like the one Farrokhzad herself grew up in.

In the poem, it is through the various family members' interaction with the courtyard garden that their individual ills, as well as their collective misery, are revealed to the reader. In this sense, the garden acts as a kind of mirror to what is, in fact, a troubled and disintegrating family – a family under siege from the onslaught of modernity and the antagonism of mistrustful neighbours, a family that bears the scars of the apparent indifference of its individual members towards one another, as well as those of their own personal problems and despair. The garden is a repository for the collective memory of the family. The garden's 'sick' state reflects the ill health of the family as a unit. Interestingly, the father has withdrawn into his own world, and spends his time reading the same two books, Ferdowsi's eleventh-century voluminous epic poem, 'Shahnameh', and Nasikh al-Tawarikh's, 'A History of the Life of the Prophet Muhammad and the Imams'.[71]

Against this backdrop, the mother is trying in vain to keep the garden (and, by extension, the family) alive by resorting to what are portrayed as outmoded tools of religious piety and ritual prayer. The mother, in fact, represents those more traditionally minded elements of the Iranian lower middle class who, in the late 1960s and 1970s, saw Twelver Shi'ism as the only force powerful enough to hold their disintegrating society together. Also present is the brother, representing a lost generation of youths who have turned their backs on the history and religion revered by their parents, and who seek solace in 'pop philosophy' and alcohol.[72] These youngsters are fundamentally disillusioned and dangerously detached from the other people around them. Finally, there is the sister, who has distanced herself from her family. She represents a newly affluent generation that has embraced an alien, consumerist attitude to life. She is portrayed as the typical 'west-toxicated' (*Gharbzadeh*) modern Iranian who has either consciously or unwittingly severed her ties with the past, thereby, in Farrokhzad's eyes, becoming worryingly rootless. At the end of this section of the poem, Farrokhzad addresses the sister's pregnancy, suggesting that mothers like her are producing children who will become the next generation of rootless people.[73] In summary, both Farrokhzad's and Daneshvar's writings convey women's hidden feelings about women's lifestyle and their domestic lives inside the home in 1960s and 1970s in Iran.

Over the past 80 years, the condition of unveiling (1936) or veiling (1979) has been violently imposed on women in Iran by the political powers. What should be remembered is that, whilst these changes in everyday living conditions took place overnight, the individual psychological and emotional response has not followed the same timeframe. Thus women of my society, including myself, typically experience a deeply rooted anxiety at the potential loss of cultural barriers, an anxiety best encapsulated in the ever present concerns about what others might think and consider to be good and bad behaviour, and which cultural norms are acceptable and which are not. The question that arises here is that, how have these sociopolitical changes (veiling/unveiling) affected women's personality?

For me personally, the fear of exposure, of really saying what I think, has been a profound struggle in terms of my writing practice. I say this because the reader should be aware of this unseen struggle, which is likely shared by many others but which has nothing to do with compulsory physical veiling since I am living in London. Rather, its origins are in the presence of an invisible veiling, a fear of being exposed and of being talked about whereby one prefers things to remain unsaid or untold, remaining in the closet so to speak. I hope this struggle is clearly and appropriately conveyed through my writing. Farzaneh Milani notes that '[w]omen have been veiled and unveiled by force but they will remain enfolded and covered by physical and psychological traces of their modes of acceptance or rejection of the veil'.[74] This description of women responding to veiling in its physical and metaphorical forms raises a very contemporary concern about veiling. I myself can very much relate to this quote, in that I live in a comparatively free society in the United Kingdom and struggle to unfold layers of immaterial veil that cloak my every behaviour.

The veil might have been forced upon me by the political/religious powers in Iran, but even away from them, the manners, behaviours and views attached to years of wearing or not wearing the covering cannot be done away with so easily, and certainly not overnight. Veiling is perhaps one of the most symbolically significant structures of a complex cultural heritage that expresses, among other things, Iran's prevailing attitude towards the self and the other.

2.2 Veiling and the Sense of Protection

Even though the most visible Islamic icon is undoubtedly the women's covering, it is crucial to note that the values expressed by veiling are not only related to a woman's concealment but to much broader moral, sexual, political, economic and aesthetic considerations on the part of both men and women. The subject of the veil is, in fact, a constant preoccupation for everyone in Iran.

The overall sense of self (the individual) in Iranian society is conditioned between an outer shell (the public self) and an inner core (the private self). Psychologically, the core is supposed to be private, stable, intimate and reliable, while the exterior is perceived to be unstable and unreliable, the domain of surfaces, corruption and worldly influences. In a practical sense, people and their feelings and behaviours are disjointed and operate in both *Zaheri* ('external') and *Bateni* ('internal') spheres. Abstractions supplant concreteness, generalities replace the specific and indirection becomes a common practice. Here, indirection is the common means of Iranian communication. In other words, Iranians will never say directly what they mean or what they want. One therefore needs to listen but, more than that, must read between the lines, since the main or real point is typically left unsaid and simply skirted around.[75] For an outsider, this form of communication can be very difficult to understand and navigate around, but it remains a very common practice within Iranian society.

This certain self-duality necessitates a boundary or barrier that, like a veil or screen, can protect the core from contamination from the outside. This boundary, which can consist of walls, words and/or veils, can mark, mask, separate and confine both women and men alike.[76] This segregation of the inner and outer space of self has been cautiously practised in various forms throughout history, such as architecture, dress, behaviour, voice, eye contact and relationships. Farzaneh Milani notes the *hijab* is also a reflection of the architectural space in an affluent Iranian home, divided between the *andaruni* ('the inner') and the *biruni* ('the outer'): both *hijab* and house contain women and children 'inside' and place men and visitors 'outside'.[77]

Considering both these physical forms of veiling, i.e., body covering and architectural walls, one can wonder how the voice, which obviously comes in an intangible non-corporeal form, can be curtained or curtailed. The boundaries created for the covering of the voice arise mainly from a set or series of rules concerning modesty. This includes using formal language and a decorous tone with people outside the family and, particularly for women, avoiding singing, boisterous laughter and, indeed, any sort of emotional outburst in public other than to express grief or anger; these are all culturally specific criteria that express a modest (veiled) voice in Iran.[78]

It seems as though, aside from the physical veil, there is also an invisible veil for both men and women in Iran, between what *is* and what *could be* seen, heard or experienced. The values that keep this invisible veil in place were established by the Islamic religion long ago, and have been protected and passed down between families (tradition) and societies (authoritative power). The strength of these values differs between families, and is dependent mostly on their social class, but for the majority of modest Muslim Iranians it is customary to be surrounded by walls and veils. An Iranian woman is expected to be constantly aware of and respect her boundaries and to keep herself protected by the interior walls of her home or by the fabric walls of her veil or covering.

In recent years, there has been a major shift in the way the veil is perceived by women. No longer solely an instrument of their segregation, it has come to facilitate women's access to the public arena and has given them a means to renegotiate boundaries. For instance, there are numerous advisory roles for women as many governors need an advisor on women's affairs, so many women use the *chador* to gain access to leadership roles in government.[79] The traditional equation of veiled/absent is no longer as clear and is not as immutable as it once was. Now a woman can be veiled and also have a public voice and presence,[80] meaning that the situation today is double-edged. There is no state of full or absolute 'veiled-ness' or 'unveiled-ness'; whether veiled or unveiled, there is a constant duality.

On the other hand, the political scientist Norma Claire Moruzzi refers to the distinct role of the veil in higher education settings in Iran, which can be categorized into three levels:

> (1) as a form of dress for young women from outside Tehran who will eventually transition to other forms of Hijab, (2) as a marker that a student is from

a poor or traditional family or (3) as a claim of social distinction for an upper class Tehrani student.

Therefore, even though it is designed to be modest clothing for all, it could potentially reveal a class hierarchy at university (and at work) if one considers the quality and cost of the veil since it could be made of very expensive silk crepe or inexpensive polyester.[81]

In comparison, inappropriate dress may be any form of covering apart from the veil that, in Islamic society, represents a sort of aesthetic or moral failure, not a successful act of women's empowerment. The improperly veiled woman, referred to as 'bad hijab', stands in opposition to the fully covered woman, a symbol of 'good hijab'. However, when it comes to the workplace, both styles 'can signal or create social distinction by taking advantage either of religious institutionalized aesthetic authority or of western aesthetic authority'.[82]

The protection zones and boundaries created by veils and walls suggest a general lack of trust between Iranian men themselves. In this sense, the veil or wall expresses their 'possession' of the particular female body concerned and, as such, their masculinity drives them to protect or hide it from other men.[83] 'Insiders' and 'outsiders' are categorized as *mahram* and *namahram* respectively. This means that fathers, brothers, husbands and uncles are allowed to see the women without the veil on but others are not. However, these traditional beliefs are no longer held by the new generation, and many youngsters have found a way to transgress all these barriers, albeit strictly underground. My visit to Tehran in 2015 differed greatly from the picture I had in my mind of my previous visits in 2012, 2013 and 2014. I encountered open and relaxed male/female relationships being conducted behind closed doors in homes and in privately run companies (as opposed to state-run companies). Parties in the lobbies of the modern tower blocks and buildings in West/North Tehran are now attended by men and women alike, who will dress up for the occasion. Comparisons can be made to London's Soho on a Saturday night, the only difference being that in Tehran, these parties take place clandestinely out of sight of the moral police.

All this makes me wonder what barriers really exist in Iran today, for it seems as though the middle-class youth is able to enjoy quite an extreme, albeit secret, private life. However, their public face, or mask perhaps, does remain quite different to their 'true self' that exists behind closed doors. When inside people's homes I was reminded of the London lifestyle, but its Islamic counterpart does continue to prevail on the streets of Tehran. Each time I visit home (Tehran) I seem to encounter more and more conflicting and bizarre combinations[84] of fashion, trends and lifestyles. For instance, one can see the cowboy-style manteau that is drawn from western fashion. However, western fashion has not been fully adopted/embraced; rather, it has been

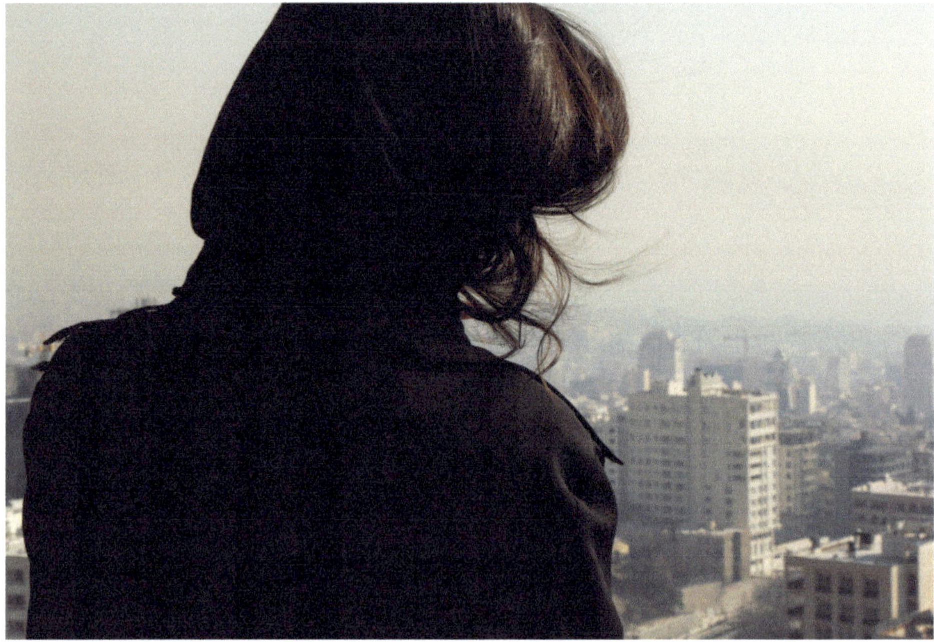

FIGURE 6: Azadeh Fatehrad (2015), Departure series. Photograph. Tehran.

adapted for the Iranian cultural context. The cowboy manteau is, therefore, worn with long baggy linen trousers and gauzy colourful *rusaris* instead of the jeans and cowboy hats that originally went with the outfit in western countries.[85] Elizabeth Bucar notes that, even though women's modest dress code is compulsory in Iran, pious fashion comes in a variety of styles. Despite conditions of intense social control and scrutiny in Tehran, one can see the remarkable ability of fashion to endure, flourish and even surprise (as with the case of the cowboy-inspired fashion).[86]

2.3 On Veiling and Modesty

In *The Wind Will Carry Us* (1999) by Iranian director Abbas Kiarostami, a group of filmmakers from Tehran goes to a small Kurdish village to make a documentary about the funeral of an elderly woman. Every day the lead character, Behzad, climbs up a hill to reach a mobile connection point to make a phone call to an anonymous authority in Tehran and report on the team's (lack of) progress. In one of these sequences, Behzad walks up to the hill and notices a workman (Yousef) digging a ditch (well) nearby – whilst we can hear his voice singing a song down the well, we do not see his face. The next day, Behzad arrives on top of the hill

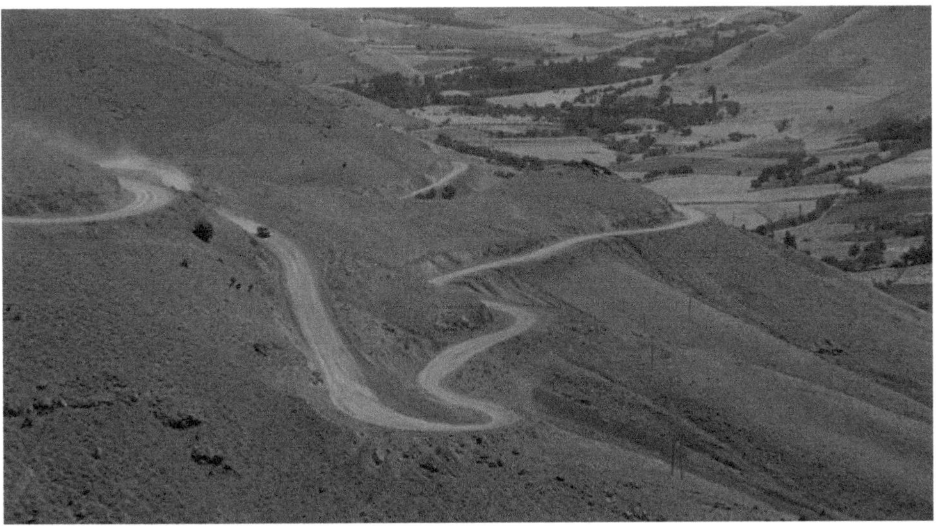

FIGURE 7: *The Wind Will Carry Us* by Abbas Kiarostami © 1999 MK2 Productions-Abbas Kiarostami. Courtesy of mk2 lms.

and notices a young girl secretly coming to visit the workman and bringing him some fresh milk, 'a substance with mischievously sexual connotations in the film'.[87]

From this point onwards, the protagonist is determined to drink the same milk from the same cow milked by the same hands. Behzad starts to search for the girl's house. After a couple of days, he finally finds it; he squeezes himself through the narrow gate and enters the yard. Asking gently if there is anyone there who can sell him some milk, he hears the sound of a cow mooing in the basement. An old lady comes forward and, with a brisk gesture, indicates the way to him. It is dark inside and he asks: 'Why is it so dark in here?' The old lady replies: 'There is a hurricane lamp; it's not so dark'. On the way he asks: 'Is there someone down there?' 'Yes', comes the reply, 'Miss Zeynab'. The old lady shouts: 'Zeynab, come here. This gentleman needs milk'.

He walks along the path to the basement and again repeats: 'It's so dark in here'. Walking along a narrow passage, he calls out: 'Is anyone here?' Zeynab appears and invites him to come in; she is holding a lamp in her hand by the dim light of which she guides him. Behzad: 'Can you milk the cow for me?', continuing 'it is so dark; how do you work in here?' Zeynab: 'I'm used to it. I work here. And you will get used to it too if you stay long enough'. Behzad: 'I'll be gone before I get used to it'. The milking room is dungeon-like, dimly lit by the small light that reveals a glimpse of Zeynab. The minimalist nature of the setting of this scene is what gives it its symbolic strength: Zeynab, Behzad, the cow and the contrast between light and darkness.

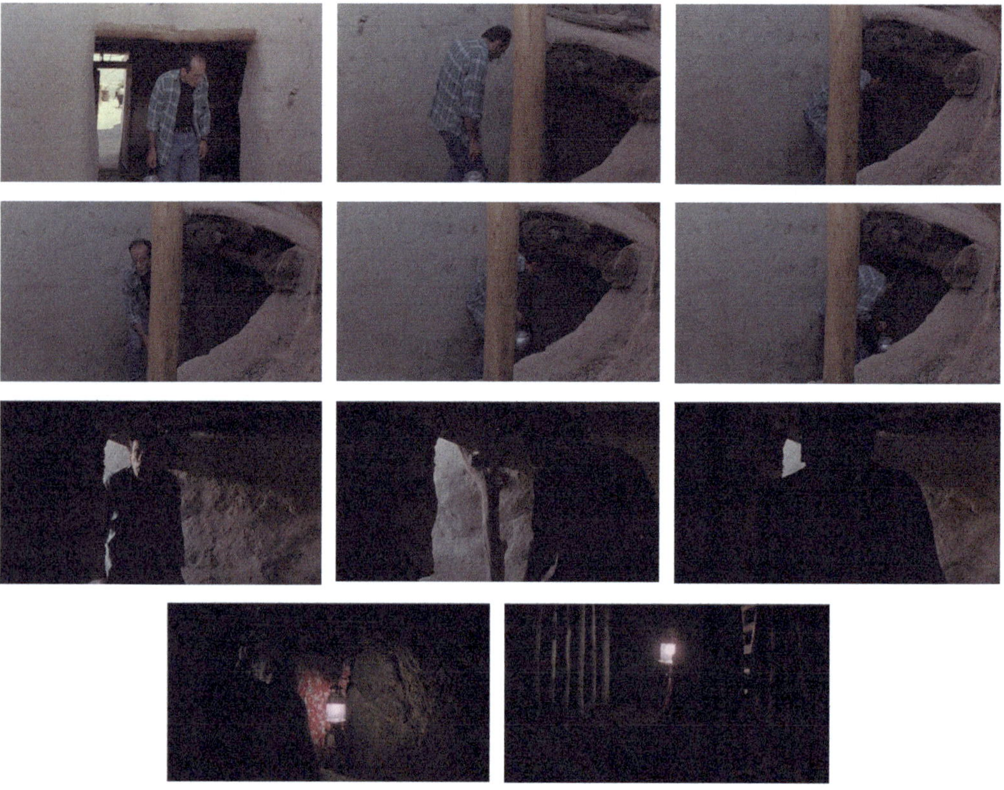

FIGURE 8: *The Wind Will Carry Us* by Abbas Kiarostami © 1999 MK2 Productions-Abbas Kiarostami. Courtesy of mk2 lms.

The dialogue in the basement continues. Zeynab explains that she has a lamp because the electricity is off, as if offering an excuse for the terrifying darkness and her rudimentary tools. Behzad unexpectedly starts to recite a line from a contemporary Iranian poem: 'If you come to my house...' Zeynab looks shocked and snaps: 'What?' Behzad: 'Oh, kind one bring me the lamp and a window through which I can watch the crowd in the happy street'. Zeynab: 'What?'. Behzad: 'Nothing. It was a poem'.

He continues talking to her and asks: 'How old are you?' Zeynab: 'Sixteen'. Behzad: 'Sixteen. Have you been to school?' Zeynab: 'Yes'. Behzad: 'For how long?' Zeynab: 'Five years'. Behzad: 'Five years. That's good. Do you know Forough?' Zeynab replies: 'Yes'. Behzad is unconvinced and tests her: 'Who is she?' Zeynab confidently replies that she is Gohar's daughter. Behzad: 'No. The one I'm talking about is a poet. What's your name?' A long uncomfortable silence lingers. This is a ghastly sequence of the seduction of an innocent peasant girl, with the character in the film appearing to exert his power against the weakest, most vulnerable and mutest subject.[88] It is like the gaze of the first world upon the third world, the powerful upon the powerless, the colonizers upon the colonized. The parallel is overwhelming.

To add insult to injury, Kiarostami chooses this hideous instance to introduce one of the most glorious poems in modern Persian history. Behzad: 'Can't you tell me your name?' When Zeynab does not respond, disappointed he mumbles: 'Okay. It doesn't matter. I will recite another poem for you instead. It will pass the time while you milk. Okay? You still won't answer me?' Behzad begins reciting the poem 'The Wind Will Carry Us' by Forough Faroukhzad as Zeynab listens:

'*In my night so brief, alas, the wind is about to meet the leaves*'. Behzad pauses and asks Zeynab: 'Do you understand that? The two are meeting. It's like when you went to meet Yousef at the well'. Zeynab repeats: 'At the well?' Behzad:

Yes. *My night so brief is filled with devastating anguish. Do you hear the whisper of the shadows? Do you understand 'the shadows'? That means darkness. This happiness feels foreign to me. I am accustomed to despair. Listen. Do you hear the whisper of the shadows? There in the night something is happening. The moon is red and anxious and clinging to this roof, that could collapse at any moment. The clouds like a crowd of mourning women await the birth of the rain. One second and then nothing. Behind this window the night trembles. And the earth stops spinning. Behind this window a stranger worries about you and me. You in your greenery. Lay your hands – those burning memories – on*

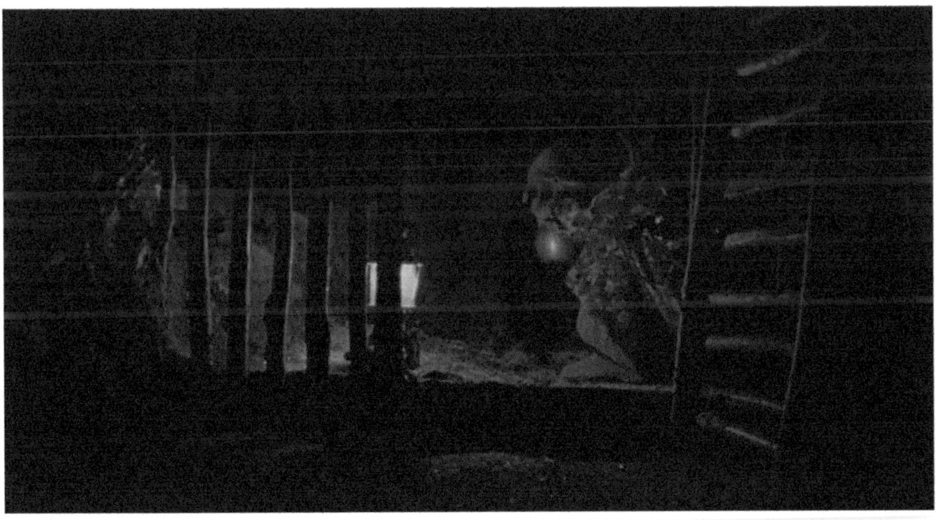

FIGURE 9: *The Wind Will Carry Us* by Abbas Kiarostami © 1999 MK2 Productions-Abbas Kiarostami. Courtesy of mk2 lms.

my loving hands. And entrust your lips replete with life's warmth to the touch of my loving lips. The wind will carry us.[89]

Zeynab is noticeably uncomfortable hearing these romantic words. She interrupts Behzad and says: 'The bowl is full'. Behzad repeats the last line: *'The wind will carry us'*. Zeynab repeats: 'The bowl is full'. Behzad realizes he has said something that he maybe should not have and tries to explain his presence by saying: 'I'm one of Yousef's friends. Actually, I'm his boss'. He becomes increasingly curious and dares to say: 'Raise the lamp so I can see your face. I haven't seen Yousef's face yet. But at least let me know his taste'. There is, of course, no response from Zeynab; her silence is her refusal. Behzad resigns himself: 'You won't tell me your name and you won't let me see your face. At least light the ground so I don't trip up'.

While all this is happening, Zeynab tries hard to complete her work as quickly as possible. Zeynab, the illiterate village girl, invisible in the darkness, finds herself the centre of the man's attention and the reluctant recipient of the poetic message of seduction. Here it is not a gaze (a male gaze) that is upon her; rather, it is words, a poem.[90] The choice of a narrow passage that enters into a milky, womb-like interior is highly sexually charged. Personally, I am not comfortable watching this scene; when doing so, I feel trapped. The nature of the interior setting of the scene, and the unpleasant presence of Behzad who intrudes on the young woman's space not only with his presence but with his words, creates an unbearable feeling. It is me, the viewer, from an Iranian cultural background who has been brought up within an Islamic code of modesty, who feels shame at this interaction – not Zeynab.

Hamid Dabashi, the Iranian film critic, sees in this sequence one of the most violent rape scenes ever depicted in cinema.[91] In Dabashi's view, Behzad enters the underground dark space where the village girl is working in darkness. He believes that the darkness is a form of protection for the shy village girl, which is attacked by Behzad's penetrative presence via the lamp he tries to shine on her. In Dabashi's reading of Behzad and Zeynab's encounter, it is Behzad who brings shame on Zeynab.

On the other hand, Joan Copjec's reading of the scene is different from Dabashi's. Copjec focuses on the poem that is recited to Zeynab, suggesting that the erotic poem by Forough Farrokhzad, 'The Wind Will Carry Us',[92] has a dramatic effect on her since she is seemingly transported out of the darkness. That is the moment when she suddenly becomes aware of herself apart from the action of milking. Copjec notes that the power of the words in the poem are such that they unexpectedly give Zeynab a strong sense of 'self'; she has never been so acutely aware of herself before.[93]

The three different readings of this scene – by myself, Dabashi and Copjec – are all related to the understanding of 'privacy', 'interiority' and 'intimacy' within

Islamic culture, and emphasize the position of the viewer of the scene. Dabashi, an Iranian man, is acutely aware of the male power exhibited when Behzad intrudes on female privacy in this scene. Copjec, meanwhile, reads the scene from a position outside a culture she is unfamiliar with. In my case, I view the scene through the eyes of a girl brought up in the Islamic system of modesty who observes the codes and settings of the scene and sees them foremost as representations of a current social reality.

In the years after the Iranian Revolution, cinema too was subjected to radical censorship. Not only did scenes showing smoking, alcohol consumption or any other practice or activity deemed un-Islamic have to be avoided, more importantly, films had to follow very strict guidelines on the representation of women. In fact, not only does a woman's figure and movement need to be concealed at all times, but the very look directed at her also has to remain veiled.[94] For this reason, post-revolutionary Iranian cinema is a composition of strange exterior shots, whether in the form of actual exteriors like urban streets or rural landscapes, or in the form of virtual exteriors – interior domestic spaces in which women remain veiled, isolated and inaccessible, free from sexual desire or expression, whether their own or that of others. Although in real life Iranian women need not and do not wear headscarves at home, in the cinematic world they are forced to don these coverings because of the presence, once again, of this extra-diegetic look that exposes them to the eyes of unrelated men in the audience. Cinema in Iran, therefore, remains covered or veiled for the viewer, who is forbidden from getting any closer to the female characters in the film. The viewer remains behind a screen and cannot see beyond it. This screen prevents the viewer from fully experiencing the story, and this stimulates the viewer's imagination and creates another narrative altogether – or at least another narrative layer.

Sexual or romantic scenes are explicitly forbidden. For example, a married couple at home would be seen entering their bedroom, but the door would immediately close behind them, and the next scene would be that of a garden or landscape. Thus, the representation of intimate relationships in post-revolutionary Iranian cinema is a highly enigmatic and mysterious phenomenon.[95]

With these limitations in place, the viewer can follow the story, but cannot grasp every nuance or layer. As mentioned previously, censorship does not allow the portrayal of a woman's body or movement or any sense of any real private life or intimacy with another person. Thus, this element of the story is left entirely up to the viewer's own imagination and interpretation. In Hollywood films, on the other hand, the viewer should feel as if they are right there in the middle of the scene experiencing it for themselves, whilst the actors, of course, act as if they are unaware of their audience. This is the magic of cinema, to make the story feel as real as possible and to make the true actor/viewer relationship as invisible as it can be. In Iranian cinema, this magic is lost as the actor/viewer relationship is constantly reinforced.[96] Women in domestic settings remain covered; it is as if they have no real private life since the viewer is forbidden from seeing this. This is, of course, completely unnatural and untrue, but censorship demands that films be shot with full consideration of the presence and gaze of the audience, meaning that the audience is unfortunately reminded of their presence and, therefore, at every step of the fantasy of the unreality of what they are seeing. Joan Copjec notes that incongruous images of headscarves in scenes of family intimacy are more than unrealistic; they are oftentimes risible, and thus filmmakers tend to avoid domestic scenes as much as possible.[97] Ultimately then, interiority is one of the most significant cinematic casualties of the introduction of the *hijab* in Iran.

The cinema of post-revolutionary Iran is, therefore, a cinema of the censorship of interiority, of intimacy. For instance, the success of Abbas Kiarostami's films in this Islamic setting lies in the fact that he tends to pull the camera back when an intimate moment takes place between a man and a woman, to separate the camera and, therefore, the viewer from the action, by inserting a distance between itself and the scene and refusing to venture forward into the private space of the characters.

Returning to the scene when Zeynab and Behzad start walking back along the passage, Zeynab suddenly asks: 'How long did she study?' Behzad: 'Who?' He seems confused. Zeynab: 'That woman whose poem you recited'. This shows some curiosity and perhaps some desire to better or improve herself. Behzad tries

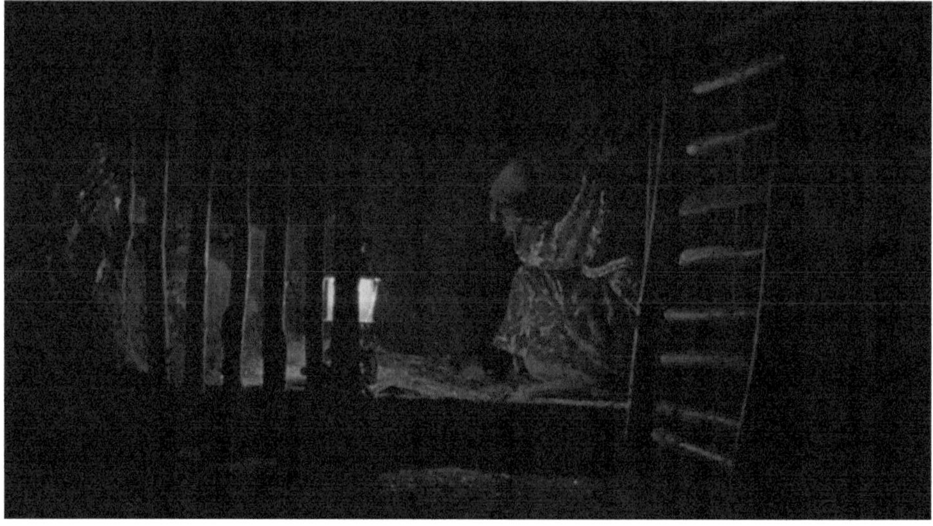

FIGURE 10: *The Wind Will Carry Us* by Abbas Kiarostami © 1999. MK2 Productions-Abbas Kiarostami. Courtesy of mk2 lms.

to encourage her interest: 'I think she was in school until fourth or fifth year. You know, writing poetry has nothing to do with a diploma. If you have talent, you can do it too'.[98]

2.4 On Looking

In public places in Iran, where genders are strictly separated and not able to interact openly with one another, the very act of looking has taken on new and interesting dimensions. Because it cannot easily be controlled and is not, in fact, subject to religious curfew, the glance has become one of the most elaborate means of communication between the sexes; indeed, a simple gaze can be fuelled with much meaning.

Segregation of the sexes is one of the primary Islamic laws to be enforced on society. Men and women are separated on public transport, in queues at the supermarket and in the overwhelming majority of other everyday life activities. The woman's body is mysteriously covered and inaccessible at all times. This strict segregation significantly charges the act of looking, so much so that it takes on a different and indeed erotic dimension. The veiled woman sees but is not fully seen herself. She maintains control of this erotic look, by denying the one who looks the spectacle of her body, thus experiencing a sense of security and empowerment.

To be deemed appropriate, the very act of looking also has to be legislated. Religious scholars such as Khomeini and Musavi Khoi have, over the years, established and refined a set of rules based on Quranic texts that provide instruction on the act of looking. In Ahkam-e Negah Kardan ('commandments for looking'), the two scholars forbid men and women from looking, with or without lustful thoughts or intentions, at naked bodies or body parts of people of the opposite sex to whom they are unrelated. In addition, men are forbidden from looking at women's hair, and women are obligated to cover it. Looking at the sexual organs of others is forbidden, whether done directly or indirectly through a glass, in a mirror, reflected in water or in film.[99]

In reality, men and women obviously look at each other all the time, with or without lust and desire, so in order to satisfy the rules of modesty, a certain accepted set of terminology has been created to refer to the first degree 'direct look' and the second degree 'averted look'. The Qur'an, which includes such advice as, 'women must reduce[100] their vision and guard their private parts and not expose their adornment in public', warns Muslims against the danger of the direct gaze – we should lower our gaze and guard our sexual organs at all times.[101] When meeting, people tend to either look down or at the other's face in an unfocused way, so as to avoid making direct eye contact. Notwithstanding this, it is common to see a person gazing at another intently until they get noticed, at which point they will quickly look away. The type of look here lies somewhere between the evasive and aggressive, furtive look. It seems that a complex system of looking is in operation here, one which is a combination of *controlling* the look and *being controlled by* the look. In this case, there is no full dominance or authority by the 'looker' over the 'looked at'.

In *Being and Nothingness*, Jean-Paul Sartre describes a man peeping through a keyhole into a room.[102] He notes that the voyeur is fully enjoying his act of looking, hidden secretly behind the door; in other words, the man is totally absorbed by what he sees in the room. Suddenly, however, he hears footsteps – and this is the point at which the situation completely changes. The man realizes that he himself may be watched, caught looking. He becomes aware of himself as being seen looking though the keyhole.[103] He – the voyeur – is looking at something he should not be looking at, such as the sexual act or a naked body. The footsteps made the voyeur conscious of the gaze upon him and produced for him the fantasy of someone's presence. Being caught looking, therefore, provokes shame in the voyeur.

In fact, the fantasy and imagination of being watched, in Sartre's text, represents the day-to-day reality in my country. We feel we are being constantly watched, whether by the police, the government or other people in Iran. I remember that when I was little I would occasionally inadvertently throw my ball over the garden wall. On one occasion, I wanted to go outside, just a few steps beyond the gate of the house, to retrieve it. My mother warned me that I had to put on something appropriate before stepping out into the street. My reply was: 'No! Mother, there is no-one there!' But she would insist that I change before going out.

Whilst it was the case that there was nobody in the street, the fact was that I was going outside the house – entering the public space – and this action, for my mother like many other adults, meant that there was always someone watching. It seems that in Iran, we internalize the idea of constant surveillance, and feel like we are continuously under the gaze ourselves even though there may well be no-one there. In the Iranian context, the 'moral police' and its avatars produce the fantasy of an omnipresent and omniscient gaze that shames she who shows what she should not be showing.

It is important to note that it is not only the authorities in Iran who regulate women's clothing, but a whole host of individuals, including family members, neighbours, shopkeepers, passengers on the bus, strangers on the street and so on. If you are not wearing a veil on the streets of Tehran, you may at any time come across a person or group who, depending on their social class and level of Islamic faith, may consider you inappropriately dressed. Indeed, alongside the authorities, 'it is also women who are policing each other through their aesthetic and moral judgments of one another'.[104] On this, Sarah, an old school friend of mine, says, 'from the heavily judgmental look of my mother when heading outside the house, I would be sure that either my make-up was too strong or my manteau too bright or colourful'. So it can be seen that Islamic beliefs with regard to dress and conduct are strongly held in Iran by individuals as well as the authorities.

Whilst the veil segregates the genders in public places, it does not isolate them completely; on the contrary, it tends to invite curiosity and voyeurism.[105] This supposedly anti-seduction device seems, at one and the same time, to facilitate the very thing it is designed to prevent. The veil emphasizes femininity, makes the woman more alluring, and by its very nature allows the mystified imagination of men free play. Dariush Shayegan notes that when a veiled woman walks gracefully, she makes herself doubly attractive to others.[106] A western woman may tend to show herself off and exhibit herself more, whereas a Muslim woman hides and conceals her body and hair, thereby cultivating men's curiosity and desire. In addition, there is a dialectical relationship between veiling and unveiling, in that which covers also reveals. In practice, women have a great deal of latitude in how they present themselves to the gaze of male onlookers, in terms of body language, eye contact, type of veil, clothing worn underneath the veil and the manner in which the veil itself is fanned open or closed at strategic moments to lure or to mask, to reveal or to conceal the face, the body or the clothing underneath.[107]

Distance and veiling are two components of the pleasure in looking, or scopophilia. Freud posited scopophilia as a libidinal drive that is contingent on distance between subject and object because 'it is through the play of distance that desire is activated'.[108] The veiled woman is hidden and distant, and functions to conceal a presence. In this way, the object of the look also tends to turn into an eroticized subject. Veiled women may thus become highly charged with sexuality, which ironically subverts the very purpose of the religious Islamic fundamentalist principles of veiling, which is avowedly to protect women from becoming sexual objects. It seems that covering women does not necessarily protect them from the outside; rather it can, in fact, draw greater attention to them.

As noted above, the constant surveillance in Iran pushes men and women into a position of permanent self-consciousness. In Iran, the state of being is to feel oneself to be constantly watched, and this situation obviously leaves no autonomy for citizens. Constantly under the absolute gaze of the state, the Iranian subject is constantly aware of her or himself. A feeling of shame requires a transformation from *unconscious* looking into *conscious* looking, of unself-consciousness to self-consciousness, as exemplified by Sartre's tale of the man at the keyhole. Copjec suggests that such heightened and sustained consciousness does not allow for the experience of shame that arises in the transition from unself-consciousness to self-consciousness. Hence, in Kiarostami's film *The Wind Will Carry Us*, it is not the gaze but the words of the poem that arouse a sense of shame in the girl.[109]

In such a totalitarian society as Iran, one's personal or private life is open to constant scrutiny and control. Iranians live their daily lives with this omnipresent feeling of being under the *gaze of the state*.[110]

In this sense they are like the prisoners in Bentham's Panopticon prison[111] who feel under constant surveillance, even when they are unable to see if their jailer is watching them from the central tower. In these circumstances, one believes that everything is seen and known, meaning that eventually there is no space for hiding: one feels completely exposed at all times. In this sense, the woman's covering offers some welcome protection, in that it creates a space belonging solely to that woman. It is a space out of sight, hidden and private, that no controlling eyes can have access to. The space under a woman's veil may paradoxically be the only space out of the reach of the totalitarian gaze.

For me personally, I experienced a very interesting shift in my understanding of the Iranian concept of looking when I came across an architectural piece by Adolf Loos, in which the concept of looking became materialized and understood in the form of interior space, as demonstrated by the images in Figures 11 to 13.

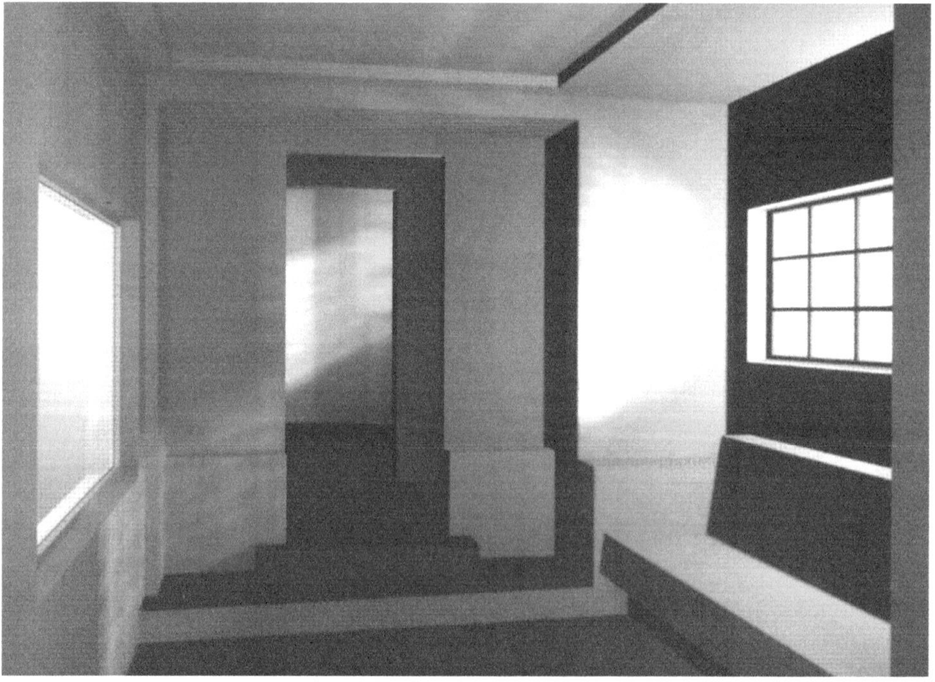

FIGURE 11: Petit Salon from Adolf Loos' design for Josephine Baker house (1928).

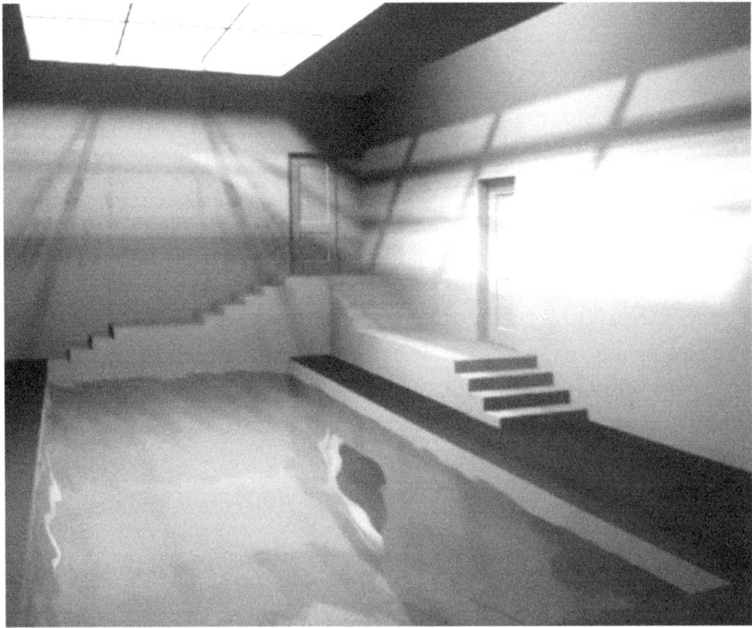

FIGURE 12: Pool with entrances from the dining room and bedroom. From Adolf Loos' design for Josephine Baker house (1928).

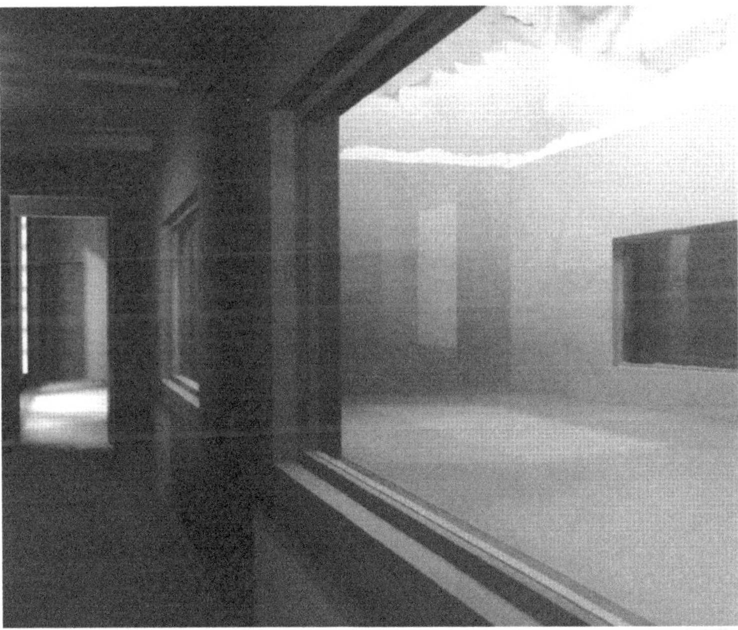

FIGURE 13: Looking at the pool through a glass window. From Adolf Loos' design for Josephine Baker house (1928).

The unbuilt house that Adolf Loos designed in 1928 for Josephine Baker actuates an unusual system of looking that presents similarities to the system of looking that I myself grew up under in Iran. Loos has placed a swimming pool at the very centre of the house, separated from it by large horizontal fixed windows. Whatever direction a visitor enters the house from, their gaze would be directed through the glass at the pool and beyond. For instance, one can be in the living room area and see, across the glazed pool, the dressing room which is on the other side of the house. However unlike in Loos' other buildings where the occupant sees before being seen, here it is the occupant who immediately becomes the object or focus of the look. In Josephine Baker's house, the visitor is invited to look through the window that frames him in the act of looking into an inner sanctum that the visitor cannot enter.[112] The swimming pool is lit from above, by a skylight, so that inside it the windows appear as reflective surfaces, impeding the swimmer's view of the visitors approaching the pool. Looking in this setting thus becomes highly fetishized. The swimmer might also see the reflection of their own slippery body framed by the window and over-layered on the disembodied eyes of the vague figure of the visitor, whose lower body is also framed and cut out by the window. Thus, as Beatriz Colomina notes in her book *Publicity and Privacy*,

> the occupant is aware of being looked at by another: a narcissistic gaze super-imposed on a voyeuristic gaze. The erotic complex of looks in which the occu-pant is suspended is inscribed in each of the four windows opening onto the swimming pool. Even if there is no-one looking through them, each window constitutes, from both sides, a gaze.[113]

The distance between subject and object that is necessary for the act of looking to take place is made tangible in Loos' use of glass and reflections. Thus, an alien-ated system of looking is created. As Oswald Ungers writes, 'entertainment in this house consists in looking, but between this gaze and its object – the body – is a screen of glass and water, which renders the body inaccessible'.[114] The position of the spectator is not fully authorized; it lies somewhere in between seeing and not seeing. It is important to note that architecture amounts to a viewing mechanism that naturally produces a subject and an object. It precedes and frames its occu-pant, in much the same way that veiled women occupy their own 'architectural space', which, in turn, creates a new system of looking.

The system of looking actuated in the architecture of Josephine Baker's house evokes aspects of the particular gaze upon the covered woman in Iranian society. The water and glass, just like the veil, function to abstract the view from direct and sustained looking, but neither veil, nor the water or glass, fully secures the body. In Iranian society, women cannot hide from, nor can they return, the gaze, which is paradoxically omnipresent and unseen, invisible as in the Josephine Baker house.

NOTES

67.   Farzaneh Milani, *Veils and Words: The Emerging Voices of Iranian Women Writers* (New York: Syracuse University Press, 1992), 235–38.

68.   Simin Daneshvar, *Savushun* (Tehran: Alborz Publishing, 1969).

69.   Dominic Parviz Brookshaw and Naser Rahimieh, *Forough Faroukhzad: Poet of Modern Iran* (London: I.B. Tauris, 2010), 34.

70.   'I Feel Sorry for the Garden', Farrokhzad's Early Poems, last modified 4 May 2004, http://wordswithoutborders.org/article/i-pity-the-garden#ixzz3Zegnv1fN.

71.   Brookshaw and Rahimieh, *Forough Faroukhzad*, 44.

72.   Ibid., 51.

73.   Ibid., 49–52.

74.   Milani, *Veils and Words*.

75.   Nima Naghibi, *Rethinking Global Sisterhood: Western Feminism and Iran* (Minneapolis: University of Minnesota Press, 2007), 39.

76.   Milani, *Veils and Words*, 8.

77.   Ibid., 235.

78.   Hamid Naficy, 'Veiled Vision/Powerful Presence: Women in Post-Revolutionary Iranian Cinema', in *Life and Art: The New Iranian Cinema*, ed. Rose Issa and Sheila Whitaker (London: NFT and BFI, 1999), 46.

79.   Elizabeth Bucar, *Pious Fashion: How Muslim Women Dress* (Cambridge: Harvard University Press, 2017), 48.

80.   Milani, *Veils and Words*, 9.

81.   Bucar, *Pious Fashion*, 49–50.

82.   Ibid.

83.   Naficy, 'Veiled Vision/Powerful Presence', 53.

84.   As another example, military jackets are worn with bright floral trousers and patent leather handbags in addition to combat boots.

85.   Bucar, *Pious Fashion*, 34.

86.   Ibid., 25.

87.   Hamid Dabashi, *Close Up: Iranian Cinema, Past, Present and Future* (New York: Verso, 2001), 253.

88.   Dabashi, *Close Up*, 253.

89.   Forough Farrokhzad, 'The Wind Will Carry Us', in *Another Birth*, trans. Ahmad Karimi Hakkak (Toronto: Mage Publishers, 1953), last accessed 20 September 2015, http://www.forughfarrokhzad.org/selectedworks/selectedworks1.php.

90.   Joan Copjec, 'The Object-Gaze: Shame, Hijab, Cinema', *Filozofski Vestnik* XXVII, no. 2 (2006): 24–27.
91.   Dabashi, *Close Up*, 251–59.
92.   Farrokhzad, 'The Wind Will Carry Us'.

> In my small night, ah, the wind has a date with the leaves of the trees
> in my small night, there is agony of destruction
> listen
> do you hear the darkness blowing?
> I look upon this bliss as a stranger
> I am addicted to my despair.
> Listen, do you hear the darkness blowing? Something is passing in the night
> the moon is restless and red
> and over this rooftop
> where crumbling is a constant fear
> clouds, like a procession of mourners
> seem to be waiting for the moment of rain.
> A moment
> and then nothing
> night shudders beyond this window
> and the earth winds to a halt
> beyond this window something unknown is watching you and me.
> Green from head to foot
> place your hands like a burning memory
> in my loving hands
> give your lips to the caresses
> of my loving lips
> like the warm perception of being
> the wind will take us
> the wind will take us.

93.   Copjec, 'The Object-Gaze', 24.
94.   Ibid, 32.
95.   In the book *A Social History of Iranian Cinema*, Hamid Naficy notes the quality of film production in this era and the representation of women. He notes that *Leila* (1997) by Dariush Mehrjui, was one of the only films that started to express a form of intimacy in couple's bedroom, and showing close-ups of her body, by using light-and-shadow reflections. Hamid Naficy, *A Social History of Iranian Cinema*, vol. 4 (London: Duke University Press, 2012), 124.
96.   Dabashi, *Close Up*, 256–57.

97. Copjec, 'The Object-Gaze', 12.

98. Extract from *The Wind Will Carry Us* (1999) by Abbas Kiarostam.

99. Naficy, *A Social History of Iranian Cinema*, 141.

100. 'Tell the believing men to reduce [some] of their vision and guard their private parts. That is purer for them. Indeed, Allah is Acquainted with what they do' 24:30.

101. 'Islamic Rules of Modesty for Women', Quran Surat al-Nur Verse 31, last accessed 4 May 2019, http://quran.com/24/31.

102. Jean-Paul Sartre, *Being and Nothingness*, trans. Hazel Barnes (New York: Washington Square Press, 1993), 369.

103. Ibid., 372.

104. Bucar, *Pious Fashion*, 25.

105. Naficy, 'Veiled Vision/Powerful Presence', 53–59.

106. Driush Shayegan, *Asiya Dar Barabar Gharb (Asia Confronting the West)* (Tehran: Amir Kabir Publishing, 1977), 29.

107. Naficy, 'Veiled Vision/Powerful Presence', 58.

108. Ibid., 60.

109. Copjec, 'The Object-Gaze', 26.

110. It is also important to mention that, in relation to the gaze of the state, there are other similar contexts globally, such as the experience of Muslims in western societies. On this, James Carr refers to the 'suspectification' of Muslims in those societies as the result of the impact of anti-Muslim discourses and heightened securitization policies. He adds:

> That has not only been discriminatory state hostility but also the stigmatization of Muslim communities as a threat in the public perception, bringing the global discourses and distal effects of the so called 'war on terror' into the proximal, lived experiences of Muslim men and women.

For more, see James Carr, *Experiences of Islamophobia: Living with Racism in the Neoliberal Era* (London: Routledge, 2015), 86.

111. Naficy, 'Veiled Vision/Powerful Presence', 60.

112. Beatriz Colomina, *Privacy and Publicity: Modern Architecture as Mass Media* (London: MIT Press, 1996), 234–81.

113. Ibid., 244.

114. Ibid., 260.

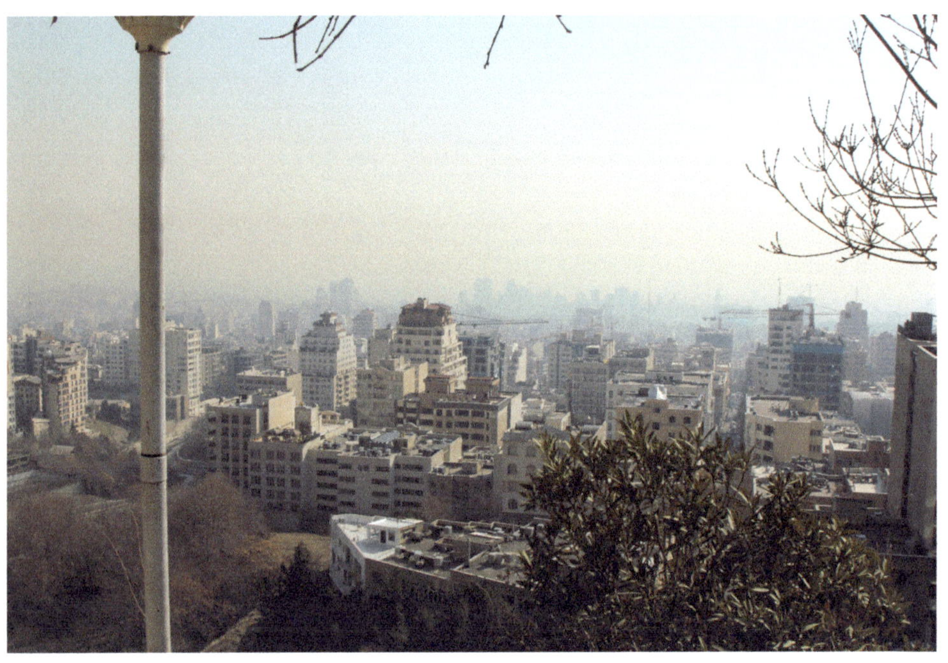

FIGURE 14: Azadeh Fatehrad (2015). *The View of My City*. Photograph. Tehran.

The strong wind is reaping havoc in the city. I have just remembered the washing is drying on the roof. I always enjoy watching the clothes dancing in the wind, but it is so strong this time that everything around me is blowing wildly and out of control. I am not sure if all my clothes will still be hanging on the line where I left them, or if some of them might have already been taken away by the wind.

I put on my coat and run upstairs. There are lots of pegs on the line without anything attached to them; yes, most of my clothes are gone. But there is one last piece, a blue garment, which is still fighting to hold on. This one was left behind for me. I try to reach the garment. I stretch my arm out. I stand on tiptoes to extend my reach, but it is too far. The wind had pulled it sharply to the edge of the roof; the peg could not hold it any longer and it fell in smooth curves. It is as if the fabric is dancing in the air as it continues on its journey towards the ground.

It is as if bubbles are forming below its surface and pushing upwards trying to escape: bubbles of air perhaps. These bubbles become waves moving through the fabric, causing it to gently sway side to side. This scene is full of movement, within the fabric itself and its descent towards the ground. I feel sad because I have lost my garment, but riveted by the dance it performs as it falls.

The fall will end once the fabric touches the ground. How beautiful this last instant is when the fabric meets the ground, so gently, so elegantly and smoothly. My garment has been carried by the wind, without resistance, trustful.

I am reminded of my childhood when my father would carry me asleep from the car to put me to bed – slowly and quietly, so as not to wake me up. He would lower my curled up body onto the bed. My bottom half would touch the mattress first; then, as he released me fully to the mattress, he would extend my legs and I would lie flat on the bed in a straight line. I remember this vividly because I was never really asleep. I would pretend to be asleep to play this game we had where he would carry me to bed in his arms. The garment has reached the ground, like a sleeping girl who was delivered quietly and gently to her bed.

Chapter Three

3.1 Mobile Architecture

The cloak worn by women in Iran is known in Persian as the *chador,* a word derived from the Turkish word *chadir*; in modern Turkish, this word means 'tent' as Çagla Hadimioglu notes.[115] In this way, the *chador* (cloak) could be seen as a kind of mobile home around the woman's body, which facilitates her movement around the city and dealings with men. In this mobile home, so to speak, women occupy a private space and yet walk around in a public space.

Reading about this private female space, I came across the French word *boudoir,* which similarly refers to a place for women only. The original meaning of *boudoir* is that of a dressing room for the sole use of a particular woman; it was forbidden for anyone else to enter this sacred space, Gen Doy notes in her book *Drapery: Classicism and Barbarism in Visual Culture.*[116] In the same way, it can be said that the cloak creates a kind of *boudoir* for the woman who wears it; in covering her body with the cloak, she is able to achieve some sense of privacy for herself, a space of her own, which is safe and embracing, and which keeps her away and protected from others. Thus, the covering is a highly intimate object, and also has protecting and comforting properties for the woman who wears it.

Similarly, the *hijab* (veil/headscarf) is determined by an Islamic conceptualization of space that is essentially moral, divided into two category of *mahrem* and *namahrem*. In this context, *mahrem* ('unlawful' or 'forbidden') refers to father, brother, uncle or a close family member whom a woman is permitted to be seen by without a veil, but they are forbidden to marry one another. In contrast, *namahrem* (or 'not *mahrem*') is categorized as any unknown man/stranger to whom women must be covered and veiled if encountered.[117] This separation and categorization of space *mahrem/namahrem* refers to who is present and occupying the space, and therefore designates which category of forbidden or permitted he belongs to. In this manner, the social space is constructed differently through veiling.

The *hijab* (veil) acts as a physical wall between the female body and the forbidden space that is occupied by unrelated men, *namahram*. Henri Lefebvre in 'moment of the production of space', describes a similar creation of space to the category that is created by veiling, as mentioned earlier.[118] Lefebvre refers to space as socially produced; it does not exist on its accord. In this context, space lies in between the 'scene' that could take place there and the 'obscene' that could not, with the two existing at the same time.[119] Lefebvre further unfolds the notion of the production of space in his text, *Theory of the Production of Space Towards a Three Dimensional Dialectic*, to recognize three forms of space – the one which is perceived, the other which is lived in and the one which is conceived. Following this line of thinking, the *chador* can be said to be a space that is produced, a space that is lived in by the woman wearing it; at the same time, while the woman is moving around in this private territory and interacting with others, her space is also being perceived and interpreted by others.

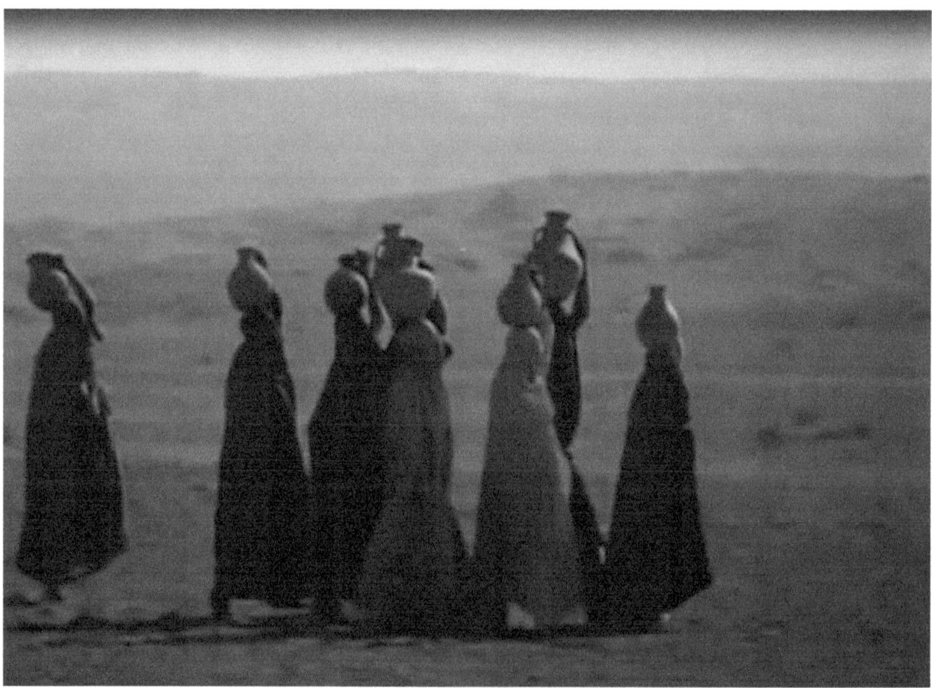

FIGURE 15: Still from the film *Kandahar* (2001) by Mohsen Makhmalbaf.

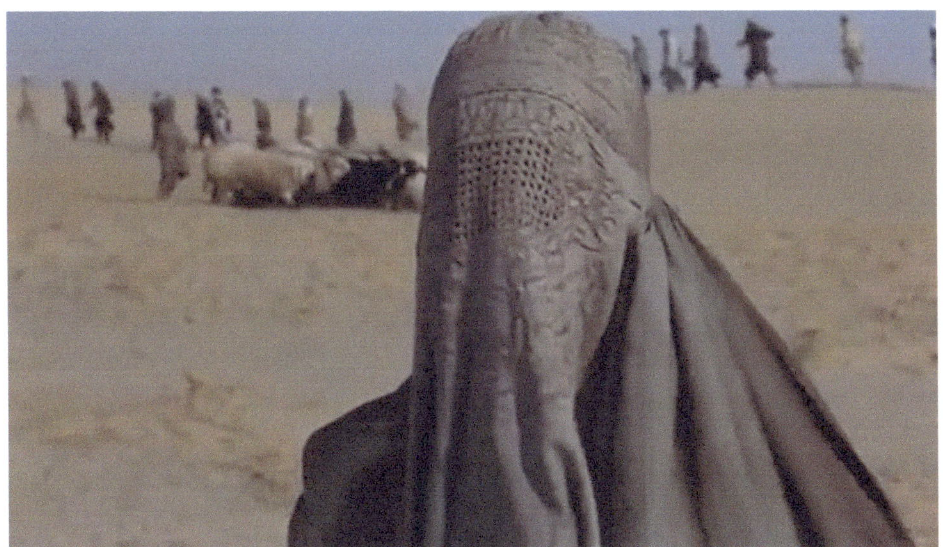

FIGURE 16: Still from the film *Kandahar* (2001) by Mohsen Makhmalbaf.

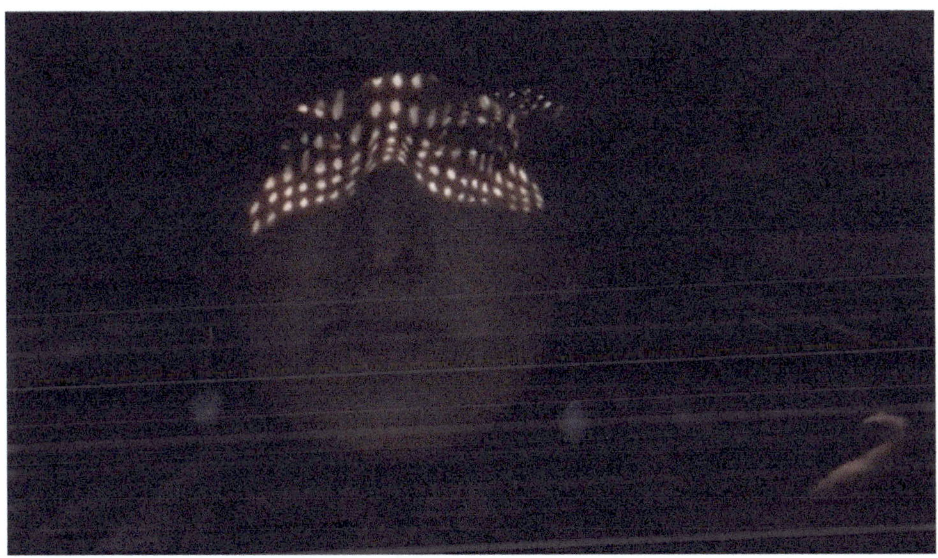

FIGURE 17: Still from the film *Kandahar* (2001) by Mohsen Makhmalbaf.

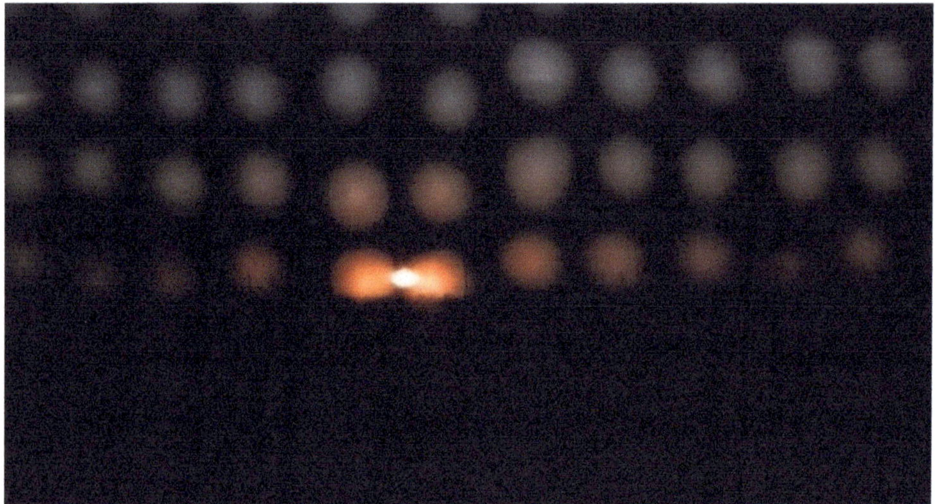

FIGURE 18: Still from the film *Kandahar* (2001) by Mohsen Makhmalbaf.

The pictures above are stills taken from one of the final scenes of the film *Kandahar* (2001), made by filmmaker Mohsen Makhmalbaf. They show the camera unexpectedly changing its position from 'outside' the veil to 'inside' it. *Kandahar* is based on the story of an Afghan-born woman who becomes a journalist in Canada, and who returns to Afghanistan in order to find her sister. In the scene, the woman joins a bridal procession on its way to Kandahar. The women wearing burqas are shown walking from town to town through the desert. Along the way, a group of Taliban militants stop the procession and start to search the women.

When it is the turn of the protagonist, the camera suddenly changes position – from without the covering to within it, now looking out from inside the woman's very own personal space. At this point, it feels as if we have knocked on a door, and someone has opened it very slightly to greet us. The Taliban militant asks the woman, '[w]ho are you?'. The woman's covering has fallen slightly; we see her eyes and the sun hitting her skin and the impression is of a very intimate moment. The woman replies, '[m]y name is Nafas. I'm the cousin of the bride'. Her eyes become the camera and we begin to see from her position. It is as if the owner of the house has closed the door behind them and is now peering out of a small window to see what is going on outside. We, the viewer, are taken into a 'forbidden' area under the veil. As with any dark and mysterious experience, we feel somewhat anxious.

I can almost feel the warmth of Nafas's breath and the beat of her heart behind the fabric under the hot sun. I sense the barrier between myself and the outside; I do not have a clear image of the outside but rather something more vaguely assembled in the form of a puzzle, as if I am looking through a tiny window.

No-one can see me, but I can see outside, albeit not clearly. I am completely inside this small room. No-one can enter this forbidden space that belongs solely to me – it is a kind of mobile home that I take with me wherever I go outside. I am hidden inside it and yet visible at the same time.

The veil/covering thus enfolds a secret space, creating a lived-in space that is separated from the outside by a piece of fabric. However, in contemporary Iranian culture, the conventional opposition between private and public space cannot be thought of solely in spatial terms. For instance, being hidden inside the veil could also bring the benefit or reward of being able to work in public office, meaning that whilst it hides or shields the woman from society, it also allows and enables her to participate in it. Gender politics and the public sphere have been two key sites of intervention on the part of both the secular Pahlavi monarchy of Iran and the religious government under the Islamic regime. During the Pahlavi dynasty, women emerged from their homes and became active members of society.

The boundary of their home was extended to the street, while at the same time their private life was, in fact, becoming more and more constrained.

Indeed if one looks more closely at the effect of urban development on Iranian society, one finds that at the beginning of the twentieth century, the average family lived in one large dwelling in extended families all under one roof. Women had access to the alleys that ran between these houses, and these alleys were semi-private spaces, neither completely inside nor outside, in which they could, and would, socialize with their neighbours. However, during Reza Shah's reign changes in housing and urban development meant that Iranian women increasingly found themselves living in smaller and smaller houses and apartments, cut off from the extended family and without access to the liminal space of the alleys for quotidian socializing. One of the consequences of Reza Shah's modernizing project, which allowed for more open and progressive gender norms that gave women access to education, work and other opportunities, was the alienation of the vast majority of conservative Iranian families who no longer recognized the new secular public sphere they found outside their door. Unsurprisingly, while a small number of Iranian women managed to benefit from the changes supposedly enacted for them, for the vast majority, these reforms were hardly liberating and family life remained fairly traditional.[120]

On the other hand, within the traditional society of Iran, for many women in post-revolutionary Iran, wearing a veil offered assurance that they would be able to access public spaces. Bullock refers to three core motivations for women entering public space veiled: (i) to seek employment; (ii) to gain respect; and (iii) to protect themselves against harassment from men. In other words, despite their Islamic right to be financially maintained by their husband, women might want to make their own income and wearing the veil allowed them to do this. At the same time, the wearing of the *hijab* in public signalled to others that they were respectable women and that their physical appearance, clothing and jewellery were not there to be judged by others.[121] This helped them to avoid being seen as sexual objects that could potentially attract predatory behaviour.

Under the Islamic totalitarian regime, private life was completely done away with for both men and women. As Iranian historian Minoo Moallem notes, while the ideal woman of the Pahlavi era was defined as being secular and modern through her accessibility and availability to the male gaze, in post-revolutionary Iran she became veiled and strictly engaged in homosociality.[122] The physical presence of women's bodies on the street nevertheless highlighted women's central right to participate in society and in the political process unfolding around them.

The feminist movement in Iran does not set tradition against modernity; rather, it believes that the two ideologies can complement each other. The authorities in Iran have always believed, however, that the feminist movement desires to westernize society and adopt foreign principles and practices. This is why the authorities have always fought against it, yet their perception is incorrect. Farzaneh Milani beautifully describes the frustration that women have felt throughout Iranian history by referencing Simin Behbahani's book *Kowli Nameh Eshq* (*Gypsy and the Letter and Love*) (1994).[123] In it, the protagonist Kowli, meaning 'Gipsy', is very much a free spirit; she is adventurous and spontaneous and not concerned with any cultural norms or traditions, effortlessly passing from one stage of womanhood to another. The Islamic regime fears that women in Iran want to be like Kowli, that they want to be visible, mobile and have a voice.

> Sing, O, Gypsy, in homage to being, sing
> To register your presence in people's ears, sing.
> O, Gypsy, with the yearning for liberty, stamp your feet,
> To receive an answer, send a message with their lips.
> There is a purpose to your existence in the scheme of things
> Draw a spark, make a fire, stamp your feet.[124]
>
> Simin Behbahani

3.2 On the Garden: Away from the Crowd

One of the most recent works by Iranian artist Shirin Neshat is a feature film called *Women Without Men* (2009). The story was originally written by the well-known Iranian writer Shahrnush Parsipur in 1989. Her novel is placed historically at the iconic juncture of the 1953 coup, engineered by the CIA and Britain, against the modernizing, secular democratic government of Mohammad

Mosaddegh. The Tudeh Party of Iran ('The Party of the Masses of Iran'; Hezb-e Tudeh Iran) is an Iranian communist party founded in 1941. With Soleiman Mohsen Eskandari as its head, the party had considerable influence in its early years and played an important role during Mosaddegh's term as prime minister, including his campaign to nationalize the Anglo-Iranian Oil Company. The crackdown that followed the 1953 coup against Mosaddegh is said to have all but 'destroyed' the party. Whilst the party still exists, it is much weaker due to the ban imposed on it by the Islamist Republic in 1979. This resulted in mass arrests in 1982, and the subsequent executions of political prisoners in 1988. Although the main concern of this contemporary novel is to picture the life of women during the 1950s, it powerfully documents the process of the political coup of Mosaddegh. In fact, one of the main characters, Munis, is involved with the left-wing group that opposes the coup: thus, through her political engagement, the broader issue of social change and female representation are shown to be indissociable.

In his book *Iranian Cinema: A Political History,* Hamid Reza Sadr presents an interesting picture of the representation of women through a history of cinema in Iran. He notes that during the 1950s, films tended to depict women as victims and second-class citizens, typically shown as having strong personalities but restricted to a life of domestic servitude.[125] According to Sadr's critical cinematic approach, *Women Without Men* follows the style of filmmaking from the 1950s, which set out to represent the real-life conditions of women. For example, Munis is kept imprisoned by her traditional, conservative Islamic brother at home; he does not

FIGURE 19: Still from the film *Women Without Men* (2009) by Shirin Neshat.

allow her to go outside the house. However, the film goes beyond the depiction of oppressive social conditions and literally creates an alternative position for women, which was quite rare at that time in 1950s. *Women Without Men* does not end with a representation of the objective condition of women, but with the affirmation of their own desire. The four women in this film rebel against their confinement, and escape to a garden outside the city. The garden here symbolizes a temporary utopian space for these four women, a private sacred space away from the crowd, far away from the city, surrounded by green land and free of other people, a space that is in the middle of nowhere, in fact.

Neshat's interpretation of the script – *Women Without Men* – begins with the sound of the call to prayer (the Azan) over a black frame. As a Muslim woman, hearing the Azan evokes many memories and sacred associations for me. I can remember the busy evenings in Tehran when I was younger, driving home during rush hour. It was sunset, and at every junction I could hear the Azan coming from the loudspeakers of local mosques. I would be listening to the car radio, but all the channels would immediately switch to the call to prayer. I can remember those times well: the setting sun and darkening sky, the sound of the Azan and the rush to get back home.

Hearing the call to prayer also reminds me of the Imam Reza shrine in Mashhad, one of the major cities of Iran. The shrine is one of the most significant mosques in Islamic architecture. As a child, I visited this holy place almost every year. The moment the Azan started was the highlight of these visits for me. From the top of the 40-metre-high golden minaret, a muezzin would call people to prayer. The giant mosque would suddenly fall silent, and the only voice was that of the muezzin which would echo through the entire place. It was loud enough

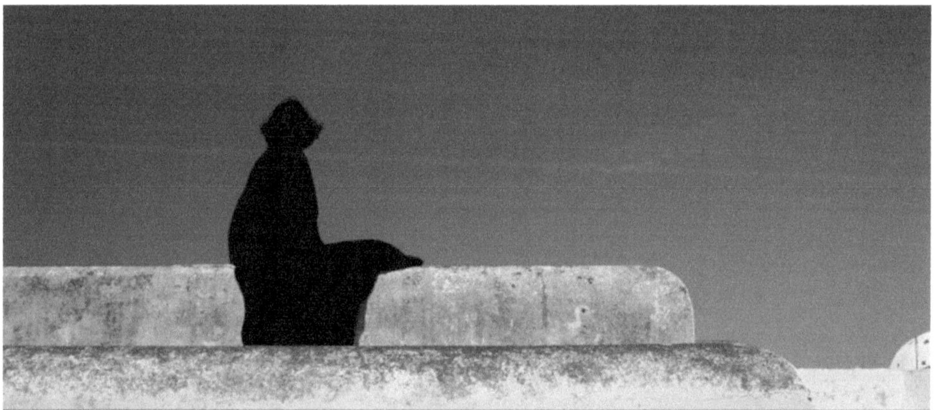

FIGURE 20: Still from the film *Women Without Men* (2009) by Shirin Neshat.

that no-one could ignore it, and one felt obliged to attend prayer. It truly was an incredibly powerful scene.

Returning to the film, to the dark frame, to the call to prayer (the Azan), the scene establishes a solemn sense of sorrow and death. The black frame evokes the black cloth worn by women at traditional funerals when the Azan and Quranic verses are recited.

I am waiting for an image to appear that would convey this expectation. After a few minutes, the dark screen dissolves slowly into an image of a standing woman cloaked in black. Most of the upper part of this image is occupied by the sky. The light, sand-coloured architecture of the roof fills the lower part of the image. The female figure is placed slightly to the right of centre, a black oval shape. Suddenly,

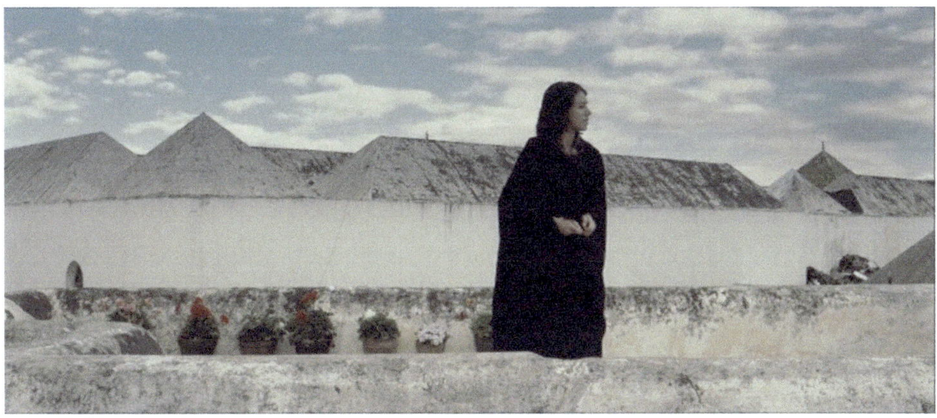

FIGURE 21: Still from the film *Women Without Men* (2009) by Shirin Neshat.

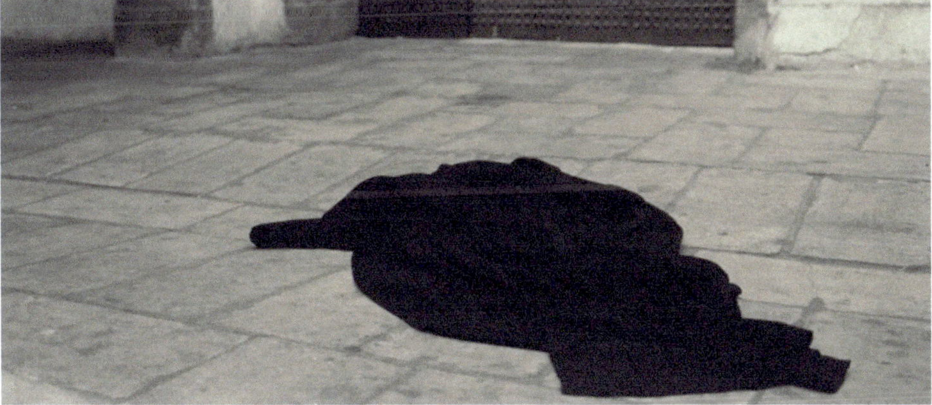

FIGURE 22: Still from the film *Women Without Men* (2009) by Shirin Neshat.

the camera pulls back to show her now pacing up and down. In the background, we see the rooftops of the neighbouring houses, suggesting a small village rather than a large city. There is nothing else to see or hear. There are a few flower pots on the rooftop terrace. The red geraniums (*shamdani*) provide the only bright colour in these otherwise subdued images. This flower, with many green leaves and a few small red or white blossoms, symbolizes rural life in Iranian literature.[126]

The woman in black is still pacing up and down. The camera takes a closer look at her hands: soft, small hands that the woman wrings anxiously. It seems that the camera is present in every corner. The woman is shown in close-up from every angle, being scrutinized. The camera observes her: from her back to her hands, her face and her covering, and it also looks from the roof at the other rooftops, and then at the ground below. It seems that the camera has taken on the role of surveillance.

Cut to a bird's eye view, looking down from the roof. After a few seconds, the woman suddenly jumps ... her figure disappears from the frame but her hair continues to dance in the wind: the gentle, smooth dance of her black hair while falling. The camera does not follow her fall but appears to remain still, witnessing instead her suspension in the air. Finally, the camera tilts downward towards the vacant pavement below: where is she? Her cloak drops heavily onto the hard stone; but where is her body? It seems that gravity has sucked her inside the ground, and her empty cloak is all that remains of her, the only evidence of her existence.

I try to understand the scene better. The woman in black jumps off the roof to the paved ground below. But instead of the expected shot of her fall and her lifeless body lying on the ground, the film offers us a few seconds of suspense during the time between stepping over the edge and hitting the ground, a brief pause between

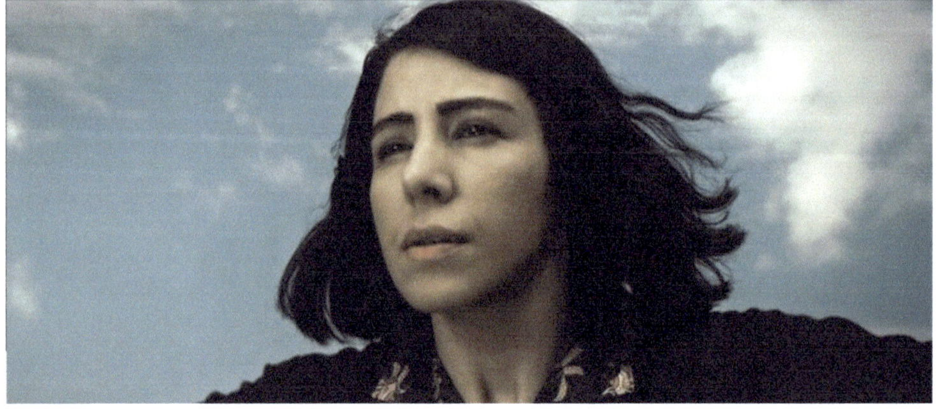

FIGURE 23: Still from the film *Women Without Men* (2009) by Shirin Neshat.

beginning and end. The temporality here depends on the power of gravity. It is as if the weight of the body has resisted this power for a brief moment of flying that ends when the cloak, now empty, touches the ground. It is as if, in its flight, the body has cast off the heavy cloak and with it its own substance.

Eventually she jumps, suddenly, and bravely. When she jumps from the roof, the sound of the call for prayer (the Azan), which could be heard throughout, suddenly stops. There is silence. And at this moment, we hear a woman's voice softly saying: 'Now I'll have silence and silence and nothing else. I thought the only way to freedom from the pain was to free myself from the world'. These words are heard over a close-up of her face. Slowly, this image dissolves into a blue sky dotted with white clouds. The clouds are floating serenely in the air, being carried slightly by the wind. Their undisturbed movement tells the story of existence: life goes on as before.

The image of the sky dissolves into a scene in a garden. A kind of 'dream life' manifests itself with this view of a misty garden. I recall the sense of an early spring morning inside a beautiful garden. Mum and Dad are talking at the breakfast table. From my bed, I can hear their voices. I do not want to completely wake up. The smell of the garden mixes with the smell of toasted bread. I should wake up. I should join the early family breakfast and go for a walk. It is so peaceful to be home. It is not that warm and the ground is still damp from last night's rain. The day is presenting itself to me: a beautiful day offering a new beginning. I can hear the birds singing in the garden. Where are they? In the trees, perched on top of the branches? They are not visible but their songs, one after the other, express their cheerful existence. The camera follows the path of a tiny river around the curve of a garden wall.

It feels like the image is not real. It seems like a heavenly garden filmed through a secret lens. In Islamic culture, the garden (*jannah*) represents the continuation of life after death for those men and women who have been good and honest human beings. It is said to be filled with different fruits and drinks, and with the most beautiful houses. No pain, hurt or sadness exists there, only pleasure and joy. The camera moves through the garden and the dream-like atmosphere. Where is the woman in black? Is she here in the garden? There is no intimation of sorrow, or evidence of death. The fluid passage from sky to garden following her sudden leap into the void suggests that a transformation has taken place. The jump from the roof has freed her and brought her a new beginning in this joyful garden.

In premodern Persian literature, there are typically three types of garden named or described. The first is a kind of royal or aristocratic walled garden, which appears predominantly in panegyric odes or 'qasidahs', which talk about the beauty and astonishing design of these gardens. The second most-featured garden is the privately owned garden, or field or meadow, that is depicted as a natural venue for convivial parties or '*majales*' at which wine and sweets are served to the accompaniment of music. The final category of garden are those with pavilions, which serve as safe meeting places for lovers in Persian romances, such as in Asad Gorgani's *Vis o Ramin* novel (from the eleventh century) or Khwaju Kermani's *Homey o Homayun novel* (from the thirteenth century).[127]

Generally speaking, the garden in Persian culture is regarded as a completely private and even sacred place. Generally located away from the hustle and bustle of the city, they are places men and women turn to for relaxation – and even transcendence – by allowing them to be close to nature and a more rustic country life. Indeed, in modern Iran, the garden is still regarded as a safe haven or sanctuary from strangers and from those seeking to exert authority or control. These privately owned gardens are, of course, located outside, but they actually function as indoor spaces, both private and intimate. In this way, it can be said that they are a kind of private room with open ceilings. The garden is a place located away from the controlling gaze.

Many urban middle-class families living in Tehran own cottages with gardens around 30 minutes drive away from the city. In Iran, the weekend is Thursday and Friday, and such people like to spend it by a river, in the mountains or in the middle of vast green lands. They relax and enjoy themselves, away from

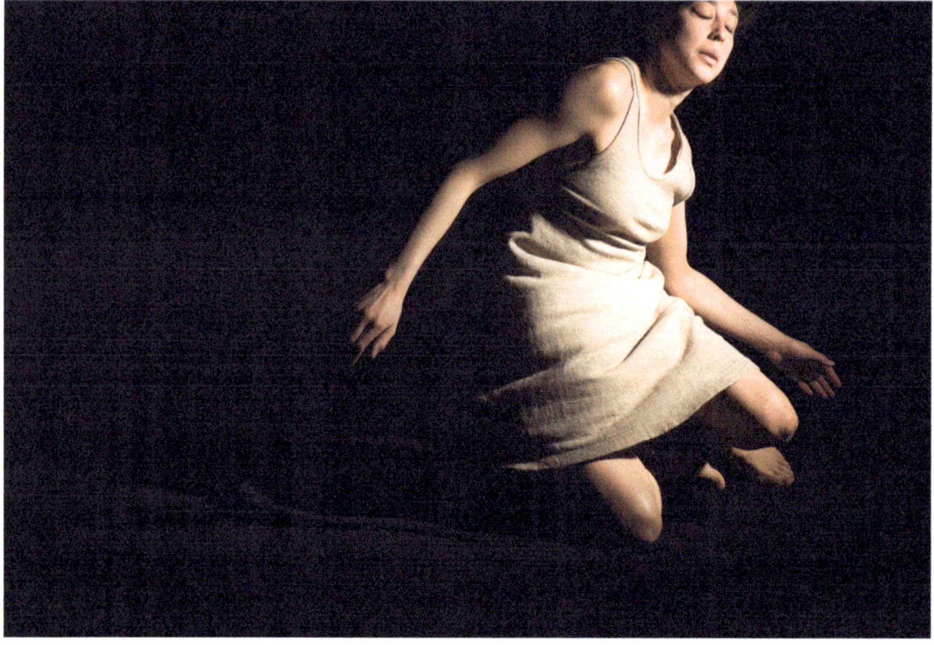

FIGURE 24: Azadeh Fatehrad, 2014. *Falling*. Photograph. London.

any controlling or judgemental gazes, reuniting with nature, reading books and involved in other similar pastimes. On Friday evening, they drive back to the city, serene and refreshed, ready for the start of the working week on Saturday. This ritual of injecting nature into urban life by staying at a country home is common practice for people of means.

Imagine this private outdoor space away from the crowded city, like a small island in the middle of the ocean, a small island that is yours alone, to be enjoyed as your own private room in any way that you like. A secret life goes on there, shielded and hidden from 'controllers'; you are free to do what you like. Cover or protection is not provided by a piece of fabric as in the case of the veil; in contrast, the space is open and uncovered and yet provides protection. A remote land, private, intimate and secret, away from the reach of controllers, away from the controlling gaze of the moral police and the prying attention of others, in which houses, which are set far apart, are just dots in an otherwise lush and green landscape.

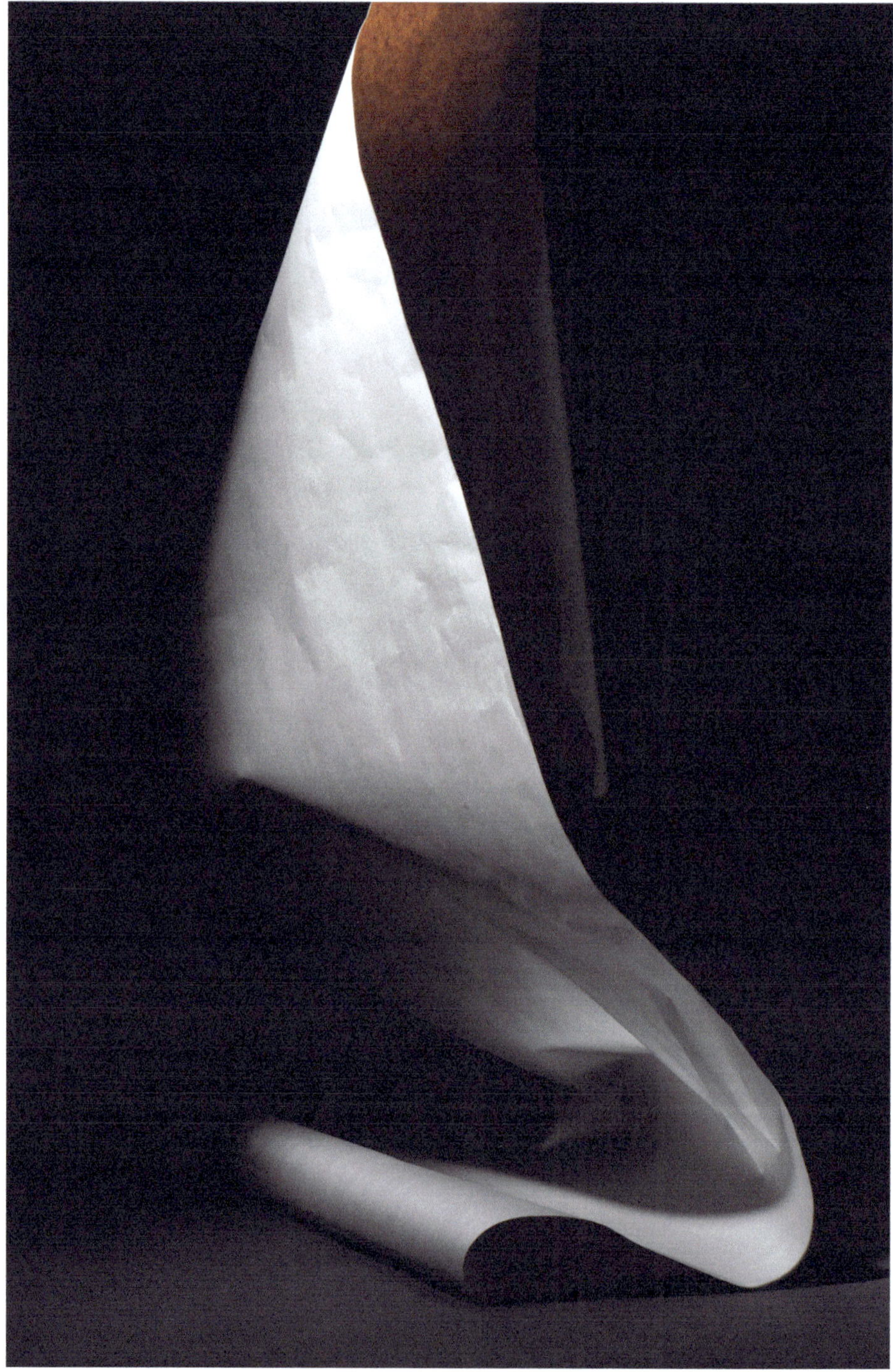

FIGURE 25: Azadeh Fatehrad, 2014. *Falling*. Photograph. London.

The body falls like a sharp knife cutting through the air trying to reach further and further down. Her limbs are moving wildly as she tries to stop her fall. She does not want to give in and let go. She is resisting the fall, but gravity sucks everything downwards like nails to a magnet. The force of gravity is irresistible; she is powerless against it. Her body continues falling, dragged downwards against the air that pulls her hair, skin and clothes sharply upwards. This strange tug of war continues until her body hits the ground. Her fall was brief and gravity quickly won the battle. Her attempts were futile. But how could you not do anything to try and stop your fall? Could you just relax your body and fly through the air?

It was a breathtaking process in a way – the war between her body and gravity. Her body hits the ground like a sack of flour – heavy and solid. Poof. It hits the ground raising dust around itself. Her body is immediately deformed by this encounter – it loses all sense of its previous shape or form. I am haunted by this shocking image of her body reaching the ground. The body no longer moves. It is a crumpled mass, twisted and broken. The fragile body violently met the mosaic floor.

I sit down to look at the body before me. It looks strangely soft and delicate – as if asleep. The right arm is curved around the head while the left arm points away from the body. The hip is slightly twisted; the right leg drawn towards the chest. It looks like such a comfortable position in one way with one leg slightly under the other. The beautiful face lies against the ground – a cold and dusty floor. Suddenly, my image of this sleeping beauty is ruined as blood starts to run from the woman's head like a small stream. I do not run to seek help; instead, I remain looking at her, transfixed by this unique and yet disturbing scene.

3.3 Drapery: Displacement from the Body to the Fabric

The image below is one of Gaëtan Gatian de Clérambault's photographs, taken in Morocco between 1918 and 1934; the photographs are taken from the online archive of the Anthropology Museum of Quai Branly in Paris.[128] Clérambault was an early-twentieth-century psychiatrist for whom drapery possessed an especially potent fascination. De Clérambault used studio photography to capture the movements of drapes that reveal the submerged movements of the body underneath the folds.

In this detail of the photograph, the texture of the fabric suggests that the cloth is heavy and rough against the skin. Looking at this image, I am reminded of my first day of school in Tehran when we all had to cover ourselves with a long garment and a thick scarf; it felt as though I could not move or even breathe under that vast layered construction. My body appeared larger in this attire than it did in my typical jeans and T-shirt. I felt bulky, weighed down and restrained, even though I was a bubbly 7-year-old girl, light and active.

In the image below, there is no sense of flatness; rather, there is a strong presence of body forms under the fabric. The right elbow of the woman in the photo traps part of the fabric under it. The shadow here suggests light coming from the top left and moving over the body. It looks like the sun is high in the sky, somewhere around noon. The woman is, in fact, standing to the right of another woman; they are very close to each other. The fabric appears to be of the same texture, as if the same vast piece of cloth covers them both.

The rough texture of the fabric suggests a sandy desert that has been captured from above the earth; strong winds have formed the lines we see. It feels hot; a very warm and rough wind scratches the skin in the middle of this dry desert, causing one to feel exhausted, dehydrated and irritated in this nowhere land of infinity, in this endless gold and sandy landscape.

In his lecture of 1924 at the École des Beaux-Arts, de Clérambault categorized a variety of forms of folds in relation to their texture and movement.[129] Here in this photo (Figures 26 and 27), according to de Clérambault's notes, the existence of 'traction and suppressed folds' is visible, especially in the centre of the image where the elbow is located. There are also a few folds on the left-hand side of the image that passively 'constrict' and, in contrast, on the right-hand side, there are a few folds that passively 'fall and rise'.[130] All of these different kinds of folds in the sepia-toned photograph have the schematic flexion of thick cloth as their common texture.

In contrast to the de Clérambault photographs that express the presence of the body underneath thick fabric, here, in a painting by Alison Watt, one can see that there is nothing behind the fabric – just an empty space, in fact. *Phantom* is the

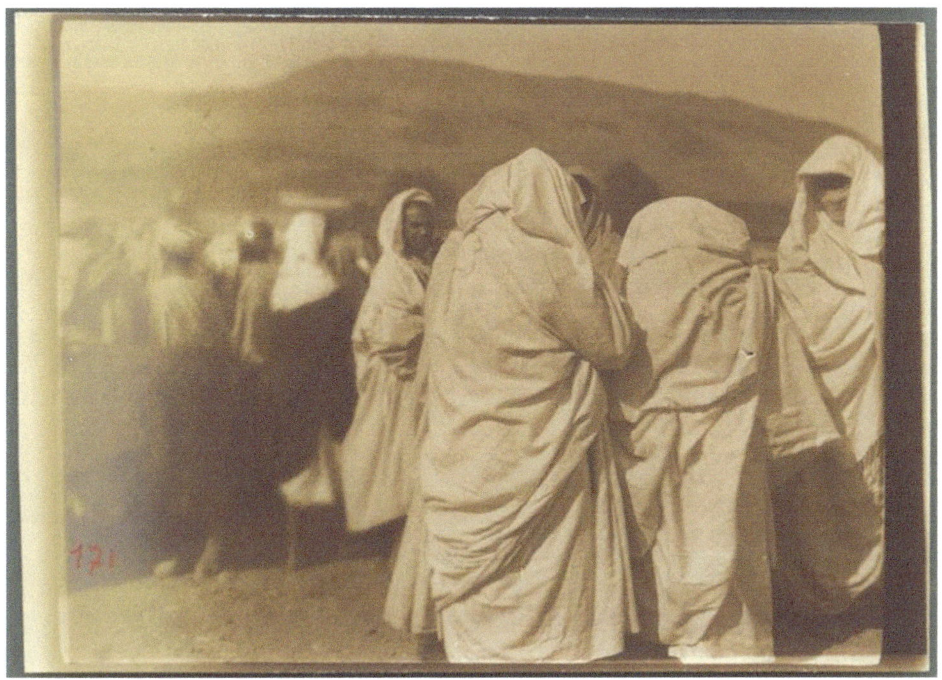

FIGURE 26: Gaëtan Gatian de Clérambault, photograph (1918–34). Museum of Quai Branly, Paris.

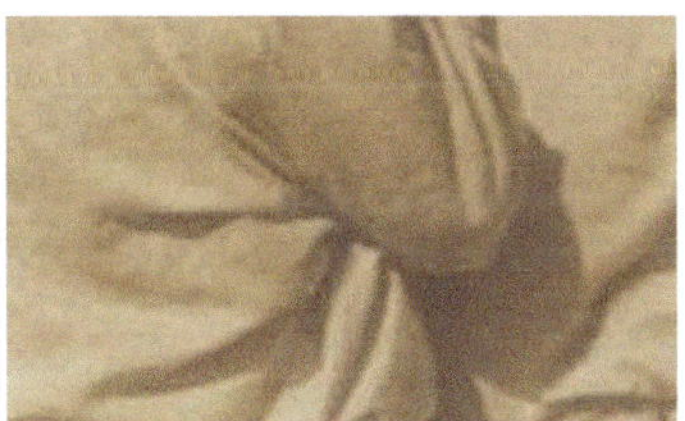

FIGURE 27: Details of Gaëtan Gatian de Clérambault, photograph (1918–34). Museum of Quai Branly, Paris.

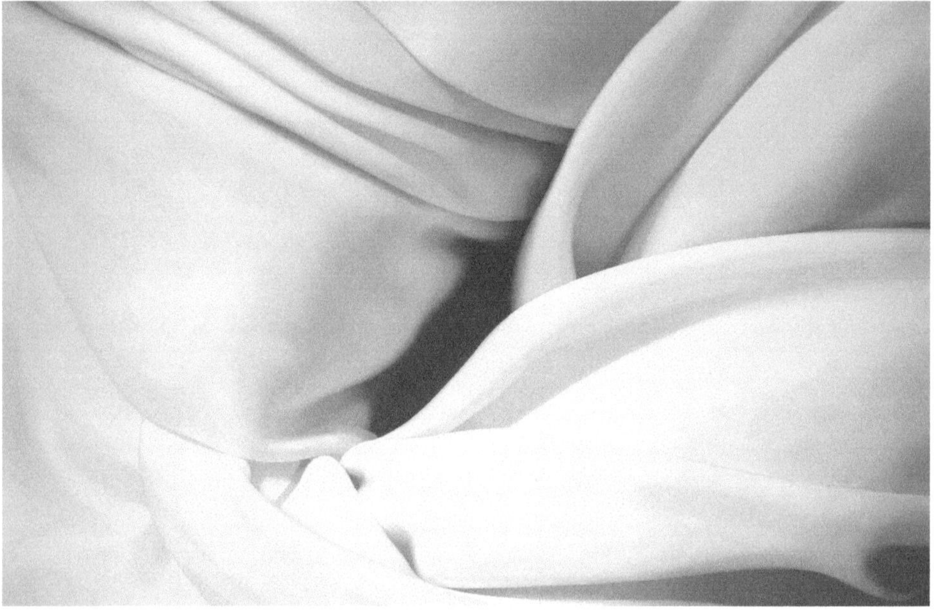

FIGURE 28: Alison Watt, *Phantom*, 2008, oil on canvas 213.4 x 335.3 cm. Glasgow Museums Collection. Courtesy the Artist and Ingleby, Edinburgh.

title of one of the paintings Watt's realized during her residency as an associate artist at the National Portrait Gallery in 2006. The white-painted sculptural fold with a dark shadowy entrance in its middle is painted over a large-scale canvas (made by attaching or joining four separate canvases together).

In contrast to Watt's earlier works, *Phantom* is not painted from a photograph or from a model, but from memory. Colin Wiggins calls this work 'an autobiographical metaphor of desire', representing Watt's childhood memory of being wrapped and enveloped inside her bedclothes – feeling warm, comfortable and secure, a lovely feeling that lived on, a kind of haunting, only to be expressed years later in *Phantom*.[131]

Phantom is no longer a material space, as one can see, but rather a negative space – a doorway between the real world and some other mystical world. The work does not suggest something tangible and physical, but rather something empty – a void that then becomes the carrier of something unseen, a presence that exists somewhere beyond the invisible and, therefore, unpaintable. *Phantom* was inspired by Zurbaran's religious painting, *Saint Francis in Meditation* (1635–39). In this picture (Figure 29), the hooded head is covered in a deep shadow; the eyes are visible in the darkness and yet invisible in the darkness, a mute presence. It is said of Zurbaran that he is the master of painting fabric, painting it as if it were a

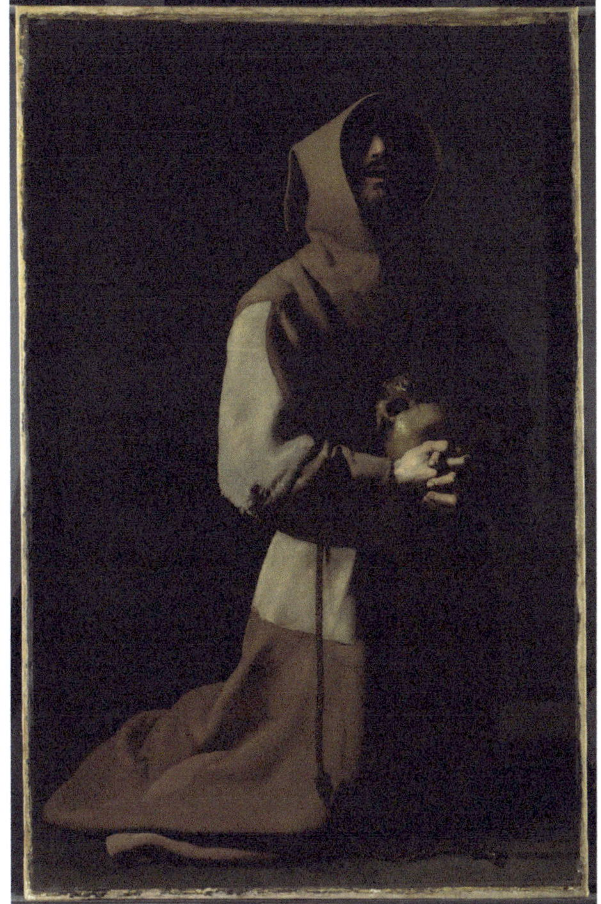

FIGURE 29: Francisco de Zubaran. *Saint Francis in Meditation* © The National Gallery, London.

curved sculpture rather than a canvas. Watt notes that Zurbaran's painted fabric has the quality of a touchable object – one is tempted to touch it, to smell it and even to listen to it. For Zurbaran, painted fabric presents a lively and material form.[132] Watt has, indeed, been inspired by this classical piece but, at the same time, departed from it for her work *Phantom*; the abstract void that expresses an invisible presence, a mysterious land, an unknown entry point and that ambiguous feature, is perhaps the most interesting part of *Phantom*.

Looking at both *Phantom* by Alison Watt and the de Clérembault photographic details, the first embodying a void and the other enveloping a fullness, the elbow of a woman, the viewer is encouraged to enjoy the vast and uneven surface of the fabric; the folds and texture entice the viewer to wonder at the quality and properties of what is before them, something that Nietzsche describes as 'adoring appearance'.[133]

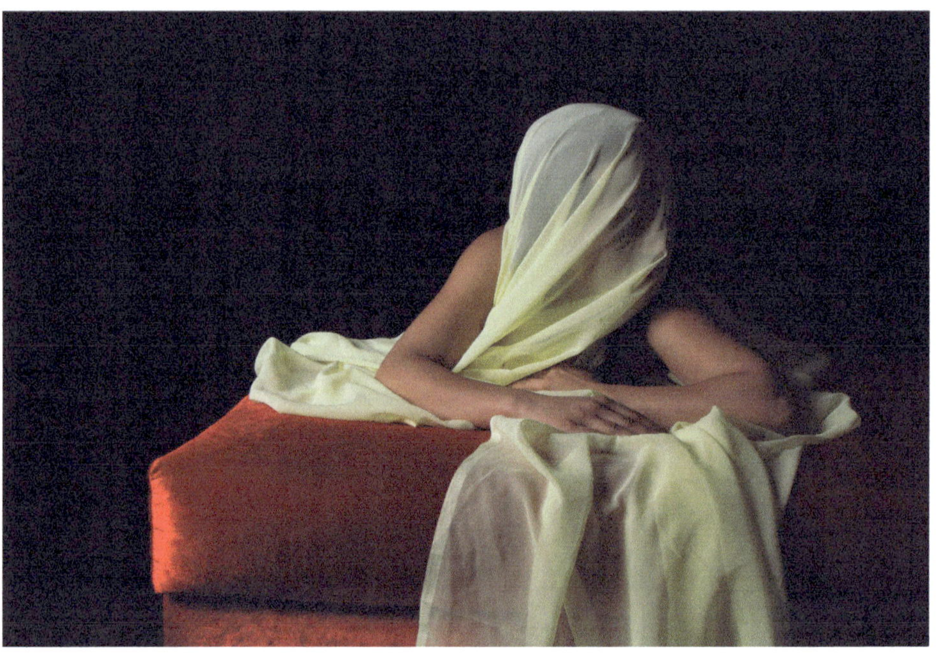

FIGURE 30: Azadeh Fatehrad (2014). Drapery series. Photograph. Tehran.

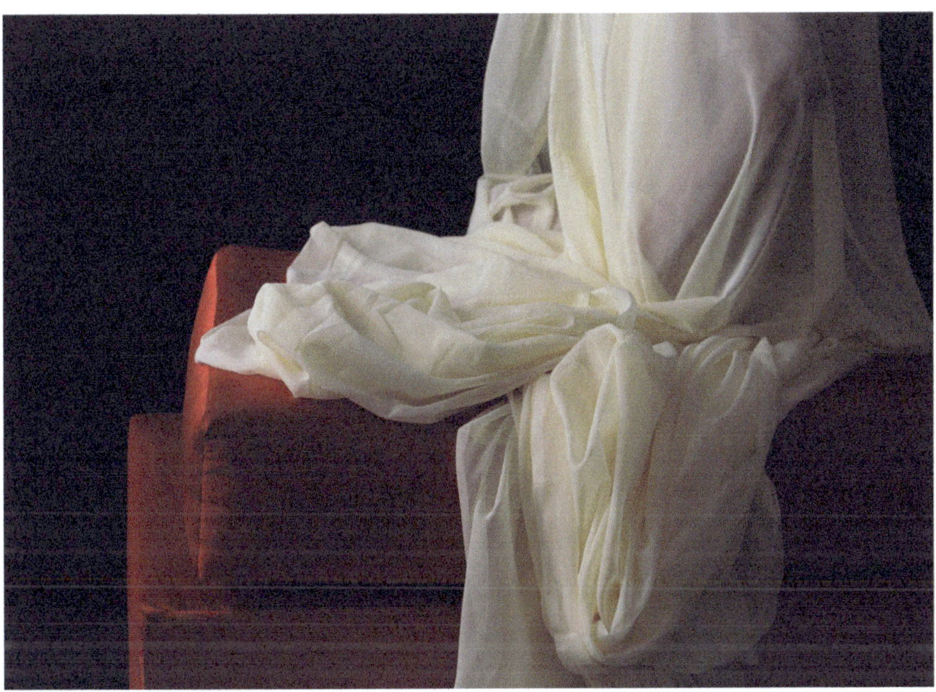

FIGURE 31: Azadeh Fatehrad (2014). Drapery series. Photograph. Tehran.

My grandmother used to sew veils by hand. She would measure, cut and tailor her own veil, and sometimes also my mother's veil. I remember this clearly. When she bought a piece of fabric, she would say, with an excited smile, 'this is going to be for the New Year'. Then a few days later, you would find her in the process of making her New Year veil. She would work slowly, but steadily. First of all, a square piece of blue fabric would be laid out on the floor to define her work space – clean and tidy. Then she would unroll the whole five metres of the new black fabric and try to find the beginning and the end of the piece. This was the most chaotic stage as folds and layers of black fabric would pile up on top of each other.

She would take hold of the top and the bottom of the fabric and carefully align them, before folding the fabric many times into a square. This was the moment when Grandmother would make her final fold, superposing one corner onto the opposite one to make a rectangular shape out of the square. This process seemed to require a great deal of concentration. It was not easy for her to do all this by herself, but she would be enjoying herself so much that no-one would dare to intervene unless specifically asked to help.

At this stage, she would cut a curve at the bottom of the triangular fold. I remember how expertly she would cut this curve. Now the moment had arrived when someone needed to put the cut-out fabric on their head so that Grandmother could make the appropriate adjustment. Usually, this would be my mother's cue to join the process and stand on a stool wearing the unfinished veil. Grandmother would have her scissors ready next to the stool. My mother would gently place the unfinished veil on her head. Sleek black oil – this is how I saw the smooth and gentle dropping of the silky fabric onto the head. The fabric would espouse her body so gracefully that I was always envious of its embrace. This was the most beautiful fall of fabric that I can remember seeing.

Last summer (2014), on one of my visits to Tehran, I came across a series of portraits by Iranian photographer Bahram Gohari. In Gohari's staged photographs, women are covered in various materials of different tones and colours – colourful silk fabric, carpet, bubble wrap, banknotes and so on. In Essence (2014) is one of Gohari's recent series of work where the veil is presented as a single vivid colour such as bright green, red, yellow or blue. The image below from the In Essence series shows the woman from her right side. The silky blue texture of the veil has settled elegantly and gently on her head and shoulders. The fabric here embraces her body in a more classical and aesthetic way; the presence of the body is certainly evident but, at the same time, little of the body is actually seen in the image.

It feels as if there is a tension between simultaneously seeing and not seeing. In the top right of the image, a hint of nose and forehead can be seen; also, in the lower part of the image, the woman's hands are partially visible as they grip the fabric. The relation between the skin of the hands and the surface of the fabric is soft and embracing, fragile and delicate. The woman's face is fully covered, making her identification difficult or impossible – she is an anonymous fashionable woman of today on the streets of Tehran in a bright blue *chador*. This coloured *chador* (sharp blue) is, in reality, never seen in the city streets. The typical colour

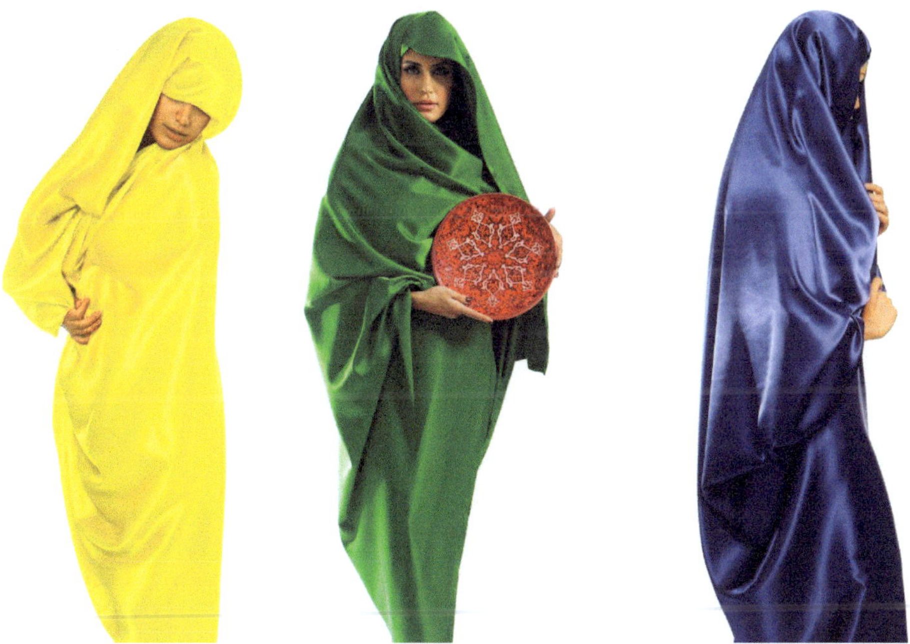

FIGURE 32: Bahram Gohari (2014). In Essence series. Photograph. Tehran.

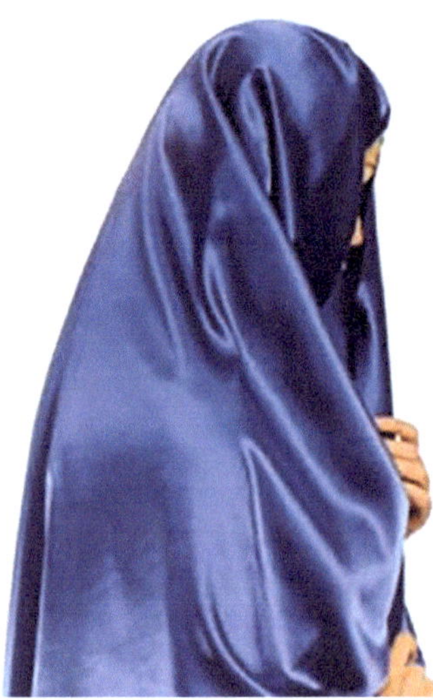

FIGURE 33: Bahram Gohari (2014). In Essence series (detail). Photograph. Tehran.

for *chador* (veil) is black in my society. The blue *chador* (veil) has never been a sign of modesty/representation of Islam in Iran throughout the history, while black has been commonly used and respected as a modest colour for covering.

Nowadays, on the streets of Tehran, one can see the Islamic urban landscape embodying different degrees of Islam in terms of women's dress code. There is an increasing mix of dress codes on the street, veiled women in black walking alongside women wearing brightly coloured garments and headscarves and heavy make-up. The black veils seen are the pure representation of the Islamic state, whereas the colourful headscarves, garments and make-up are an indication of the processes of re-interpretation and appropriation of the dress codes that were originally set by the Islamic state. All these different ways of wearing the covering/*hijab* come to represent an aspect of the Islamic urban space in which, as suggested by Gohari's photograph, a tension between concealing and showing, seeing and not seeing is expressed. Women are not fully exposed, but they are partly exposed. There is no clear Islamic and non-Islamic dress code in these fashionable clothing; rather all dress codes seen are a version or expression of the Islamic dress code, creating different shades of grey rather than simply black or white.

It is important to note here that the grey scale of appropriate or inappropriate fashion is defined by the local culture. For instance, the same item of clothing in Iran might be considered sexually provocative due to how tight/fitted it is and how much skin it exposes, whereas it might draw no attention at all and be considered

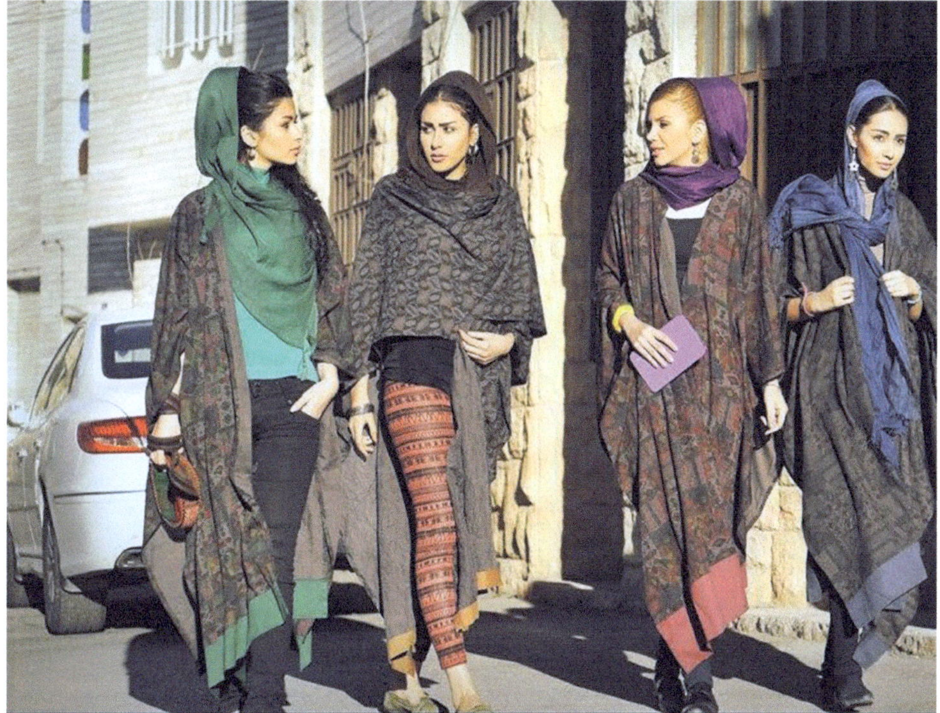

FIGURE 34: Online found image of women in Iran (2015).

entirely normal in the United Kingdom.[134] While western countries may adopt very relaxed approaches to clothing, some degree of basic coverage is deemed essential within an Islamic fundamentalist context. The modest Islamic dress code demands the covering of the 'private parts' of women, which refers to the entire body save for the feet and ankles, the hands and wrists, and the face; the rest of the body including the hair is all considered private and must be covered by fabric.

Before hiding from sight like an opaque veil,
before letting light through like a translucent veil
before showing the thing like a transparent veil
before hinting to sight like a veil that lets one make out, through the diapha-
nous light, the thing and the forms it is embracing,
before all else, my tallith touches itself.

Before this and before that… that is how your presence speaks to me.
Before all else, my tallith touches itself – my shawl touches itself on layers of
organic curvy folds on top of each other.[135]

3.4 Today in Iran: The Contemporary Public Life

The restrictions on clothing for women in Iran is based on governmental 'authoritative politics', which turns fashion into a political statement.[136] Frantz Fanon notes that one of the most significant elements of Muslim society is the act of veiling for women.[137] Visitors to a Muslim country may not necessarily be aware that Muslims do not consume pork, or that Muslims avoid sexual relations during Ramadan but, for the majority, it is the veiling of women that represents and symbolizes Islamic culture.[138] Veiling, therefore, is a clear and distinctive political statement in Muslim society.

Elizabeth Bucar notes that, while the state imposes a dress code on women, it has become a way to control the direction of modernization and development in post-revolutionary Iran, for women have created new styles of dress that could allow them to remain publicly Muslim while still abiding by new political restrictions on full-body covering.[139] She adds that some western journalists and scholars have portrayed 'bad hijab' as a counter-movement, an act of resistance to the regime's authority, which I have also thought during my lifetime in Iran and abroad. However, I realized after reading more on the subject that this interpretation is problematic. The aesthetic of the 'bad hijab' is surely different from the veiled body and it is 'political insofar as it challenges existing aesthetic preferences and officially promoted moral values, even if only on an ad hoc basis'.[140] Bucar notes that, even though many elements of secular fashion are expressed in bad hijab's agency (high heels, side slits, glamorous make-up, denim), it is unlikely that we could conclude that 'bad hijab' is part of a coordinated feminist revolution.[141] We can argue here that Iranian women of today are appropriating the most visible political statement at their disposal, i.e., clothing.

Hengameh Golestan's photograph (Figure 36) is a key image that heralds 'an aesthetic of resistance' in Iranian feminist history. As previously mentioned, this photograph was taken on 8 March 1979, just a few weeks after the revolution, when the new government announced the compulsory dress code for women. The second image (Figure 37) suggests that women of today's Iran publicly express their resistance in the form of an aesthetic rather than actual protest, appropriating the object of oppression and turning it into an object of aesthetic pleasure. It is interesting to note that the *hijab*/scarf, which is the primary signifier of the Muslim faith in the field of visibilities, is now turned into an *accessory*, that is, something that can be added to and which complements an outfit.

The dress code is strictly enforced by the ruling Government of the Islamic Republic of Iran, which has been in power since the Iranian Revolution of 1979. There is a specific governmental section that is dedicated to the enforcement of the *hijab* called Sazman-e Basij-e Mostaz'afan or The Organisation for the Mobilisation of

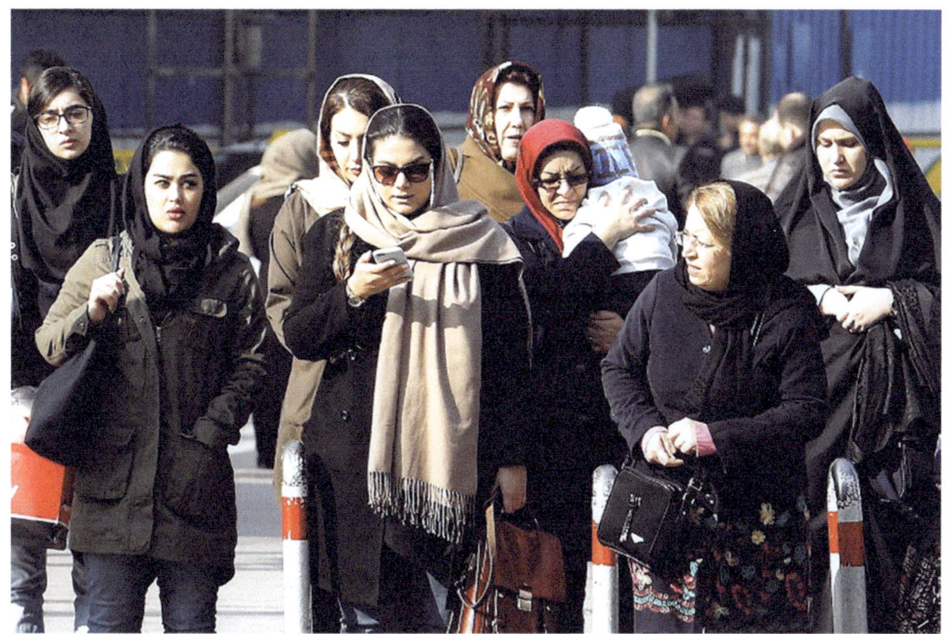

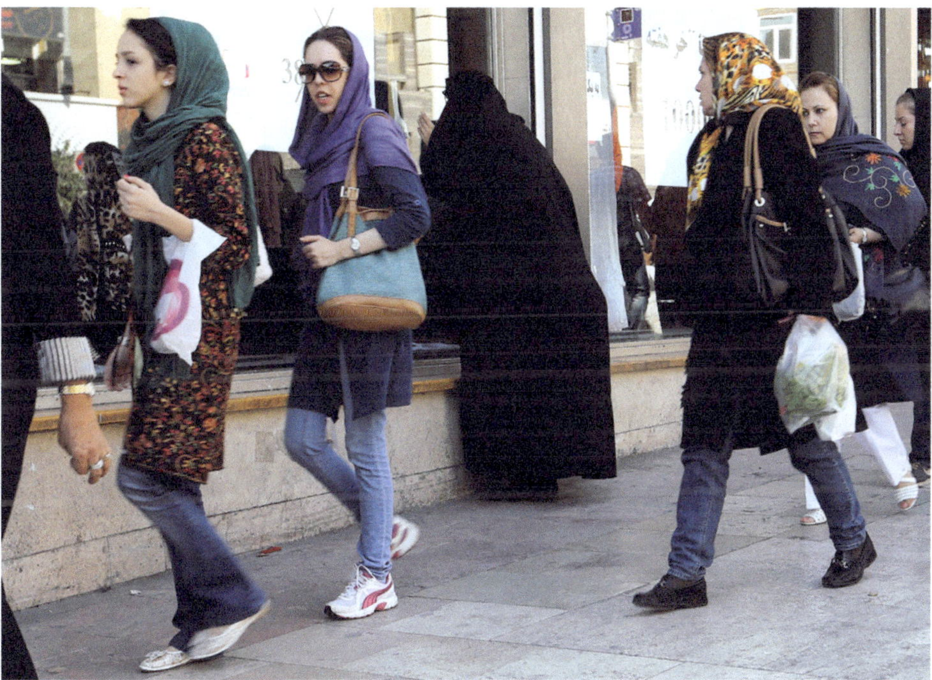

FIGURE 35: Online found images of women in Tehran, Iran (2014).

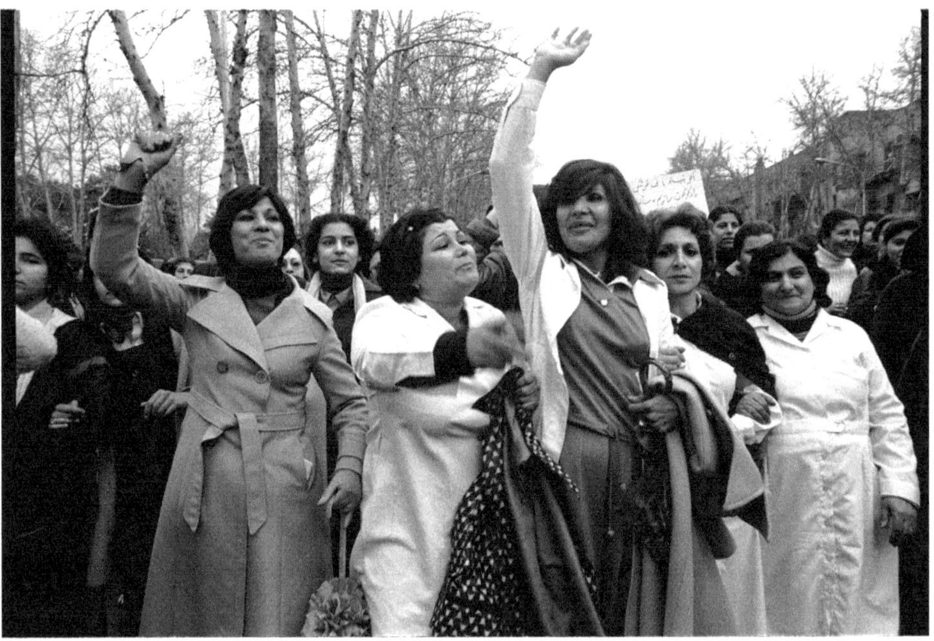

FIGURE 36: Hengameh Golestan, Untitled (Witness '79 series) © Hengameh Golestan.

the Oppressed (the Basij).[142] This was founded at the start of the Islamic Republic by Ayatollah Khomeini and consists of volunteer members of the Iranian Revolutionary Guards. Elizabeth Bucar notes that these men harass and shame women and girls they consider to be in violation of the strict Islamic dress code. Their mission is to assure absolute adherence to Islamic values in public spaces in Iran at all times and that includes the policing of the appropriate wearing of the veil.[143] They have the power to arrest women for various reasons, but it will generally be because of five main categories of offence: exposure, sloppy dress, western clothing, improper head covering and heavy make-up.[144]

Iranian women are frequently accused of violating the strict Islamic dress code. There are five entities that have a part to play in terms of Islamic values in so far as they relate to women's dress code and pious fashion: the clergy/religious leaders, the Basij (moral police), advertising/propaganda, fashion designers and fashion blogs.[145] These five groups/things influence the fashion that appears on the streets of Iran; sometimes they agree with each other, but more often than not they offer opposing views. For instance, Mahla Zamani launched *Lotus: A Persian Quarterly* in 2001, which became the first Iranian magazine since the establishment of the Islamic Republic to show the faces of women.[146] The magazine has to some degree followed Islamic law/convention in order to be able to launch publicly and yet it would not be approved by the powers that be;

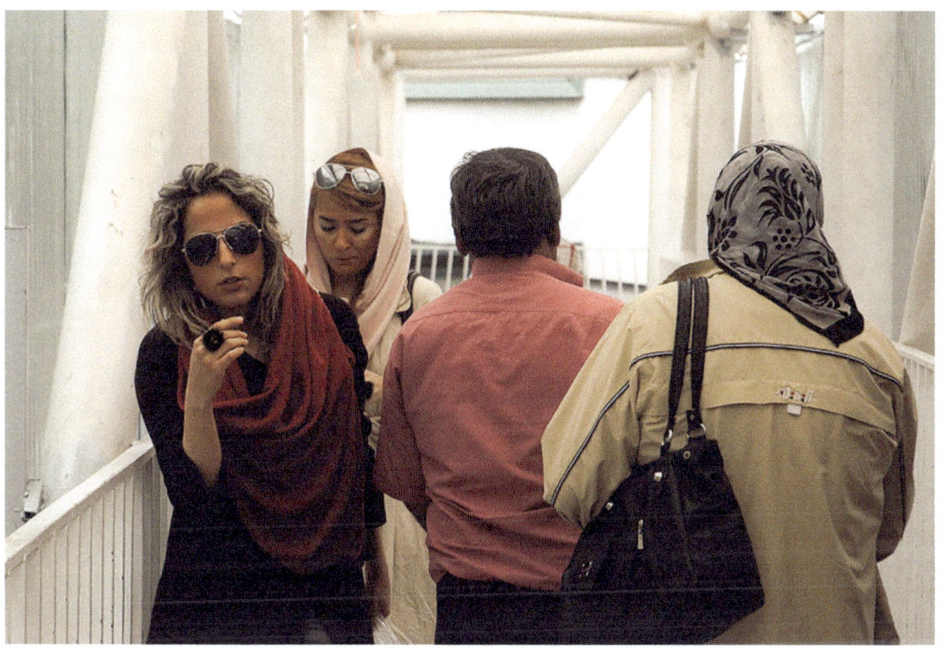

FIGURE 37: Online found image of women in Street of Tehran (2015).

therefore, many bookshops do not sell the magazine and publishing grants are generally not available to it. At the same time, Araz Fazaeli founded the first Iranian blog on street fashion, The Tehran Times,[147] which showcases street style. Even though the platform is located online, the images of stylishly dressed girls on the streets of Tehran are not appropriate as far as the religious leaders and moral police are concerned, and it would not be a surprise if the blog's server suddenly went down overnight.

In his book, *The Problem of Hijab* (1974), Iranian Islamic philosopher Morteza Motahhari states that men are driven by sexual instincts and are incapable of controlling their sex drive. Their sexual appetite necessitates women's veiling in order to preserve their honour.[148] It seems that Islamic fundamentalism justifies veiling as a protection of the woman's body from the gaze of men, as a shield to reduce the sexual tension in the public sphere of society. From this perspective, veiling represents the power and authority of the Muslim male elite.

It is important to address the fact that the veil in Iran is as much about religion as it is a westernization and modernity dilemma. It was discussed earlier in this book that the dress code was one of the very first elements to be used by the clergy in Iran to showcase their power and opposition to the westernized Pahlavi dynasty, for it is fundamentally against the 'westoxivation' of society (*gharbzadegi*). The fascinating term 'westoxivation' was coined when the legendary Iranian writer Jalal Al-e-Ahmad referred to the dramatic cultural situation under Mohammad Reza Shah that indicated the loss of Iranian culture in favour of western values. More recently, Mostafa Pourmohammadi, the Iranian Interior Minister (2005–08), stated: 'When the "Muslim dress code" comes under attack, it is our duty to protect this most valuable cultural treasure'.[149] It was inevitable that 'the bareheaded woman dressed in a mini skirt represents all Iranian social ills, while a woman in modest clothing is an antidote against past Western cultural invasions, as well as inoculation to protect against future ones'.[150]

Masserat Amir-Ebrahimi, a noted Iranian feminist and sociologist, remarks, '[i]n the past two decades, gradual transgressions of Urf and Shari'a have become a sign of modernity and resistance for many women and young people who wish to generate changes in their situation'.[151] She further explains that,

> If 'improperly veiled' women in urban public spaces are considered a challenge to Shari'a and the rules of public conduct in the Islamic Republic, the acts of self-narration and self-disclosure in 'Weblogistan' are considered a transgression of Urf and the rules of patriarchy.[152]

Transgressing *urf*, a common practice among urban middle-class women and youths, refers to resisting the Islamization of society. The English sociologist Chris

Jenks defines transgression as 'that conduct which breaks rules or exceeds boundaries'.[153] As such, he considers it an indicator of modernity:

> A feature of modernity, accelerating into postmodernity, is the desire to transcend limits – limits that are physical, racial, aesthetic, sexual, national, legal and moral [...] Modernity has unintentionally generated an ungoverned desire to extend, exceed, or go beyond the margins of acceptability or normal performance.[154]

Even though women are fighting on this common and shared Web platform, the movement is more or less based upon individual acts of pushing these boundaries and restrictions. In both, a woman expresses/exposes herself publicly. Through both, an absence becomes a presence. Both are a means of expression and communication: 'one gives her voice a body, the other gives her body a voice'.[155]

According to Masserat Amir-Ebrahimi, there are four generations of Iranians. The first generation was born in the 1930s, fought for the Iranian Revolution and had the full experience of both the Pahlavi and Islamic Revolution lifestyles. The second generation was born in the 1960s, and is described as the *burnt generation*; they are those who struggled with the moral police to, amongst other things, wear jeans and trainers. They also lived through the Iran-Iraq War. The third generation was born in the 1980s, and they are the political generation of Iranians. They are well-informed and well-connected, largely due to the Internet, and exhibit more liberal views and behaviours. In fact, during the 1980s, a secret private life emerged in Iran, with people building cinemas in their basement and holding parties. The most recent generation is those born in the 1990s and beyond. Typically, they are only children and have been rather coddled and indulged by their parents. They are the most challenging and difficult to control generation in Iran. A significant development and support was provided by Gholamhossein Karbaschi, mayor of Tehran, between 1988 and 1998, who established many cultural centres around Tehran, to encourage the involvement of younger generations in cultural activities such as art, literature and theatre. On the other hand, Mohammad Khatami was president of Iran during 1997–2005 and continued these developments and achieved significant cultural and sociopolitical progress both domestically and globally.

In the establishment of Islamic dress code in 1979 there was no clear outline of exact dress code but somehow a vague description of modest clothing that could be interpreted and modified over years. As a result, today, Iranian women have some degree of 'choice in what they wear even if multiple authorities – individuals, institutions, organizations – attempt to influence or coerce that decision'.[156]

NOTES

115. Çagla Hadimioglu, 'Black Tent', TEXT Revue, 2010, last accessed 12 November 2015, http://www.text-revue.net/revue/heft-8/black-tents/text.

116. Gen Doy, *Drapery: Classicism and Barbarism in Visual Culture* (London: I.B. Tauris, 2001), 195.

117. Çagla Hadimioglu, 'Black Tent'.

118. Ibid.

119. Christian Schmid, 'Henry Lefebvre: Theory of the Production of Space Towards a Three Dimensional Dialectic', in *Space, Difference, Everyday Life: Reading Henry Lefebvre*, eds. Kanishka Goonewardena, Stefan Kipfer, Richard Milgrom and Christian Schmid (London: Routledge, 2008), 27–30.

120. For more details, see Homa Hoodfar, *Return to the Veil: Personal Strategy and Public Participation in Egypt* (London: Routledge, 1991), 119; Arlene E. Macleod, *Accommodating Protest: Working Women, the New Veiling, and Change in Cairo* (New York: Columbia University Press, 1993), 110.

121. Katherine Bullock, *Rethinking Muslim Women and the Veil: Challenging Historical and Modern Stereotypes* (Herndon: International Institute of Islamic Thought, 2007), 99.

122. In sociology, *homosociality* means same-sex relationships that are not of a romantic or sexual nature, such as friendship, mentorship or others. The opposite of *homosocial* is heterosocial, preferring non-sexual relations with the opposite sex. Minoo Moallem, *Between Warrior Brother and Veiled Sister* (Berkeley: University of California Press, 2005), 115.

123. Farzaneh Milani, *Veils and Words: The Emerging Voices of Iranian Women Writers* (New York: Syracuse University Press, 1992), 235–39.

124. Ibid., 238.

125. Hamid Reza Sadr, *Iranian Cinema: A Political History* (London: I.B. Tauris, 2006), 257.

126. The writer Sohrab Sepehri uses his drawings of *shamdani* pots as a symbol of country life in many of his poems.

127. Dominic Parviz Brookshaw and Naser Rahimieh, *Forough Faroukhzad: Poet of Modern Iran* (London: I.B. Tauris, 2010), 44.

128. 'Anthropology Museum of Quai Branlyin Paris', de Clérambault's work, last accessed 1 October 2015, http://collections.quaibranly.fr/#0bf65ffc-9f7b-414d-81e1-a8ef93292c83.

129. Doy, *Drapery*, 119.

130. Ibid., 120.

131. Colin Wiggins, *Alison Watt: Phantom* (London: National Gallery, 2008), 20.

132. Ibid., 22.

133. 'Oh, those Greeks! They knew how to live. What is required for that is to stop courageously at the surface, the fold, the skin, *to adore appearance*, to believe in forms, tones, words, in the whole Olympus of appearance'. Doy, *Drapery*, 153, emphasis added.

134. Elizabeth Bucar, *Pious Fashion: How Muslim Women Dress* (Cambridge: Harvard University Press, 2017).

135. A shawl with a ritually knotted fringe at each of the four corners traditionally worn by Jewish males, especially at morning prayer. Also called the *prayer shawl*. Hélène Cixous and Jacques Derrida, *Veils: Cultural Memory in the Present* (Palo Alto: Stanford University Press, 2001), 64.

136. Jennifer Craik, *Fashion: The Key Concepts* (Oxford: Berg, 2009), 42.

137. Frantz Fanon, *A Dying Colonialism* (New York: Grove Press, 1967), 162.

138. Ibid.

139. Bucar, *Pious Fashion*, 26–27.

140. Ibid., 53–54.

141. Ibid.

142. Ibid., 59.

143. Ibid.

144. Ibid., 53.

145. Ibid., 55.

146. Ibid., 65.

147. 'Tehran's Street Styles', The Tehran Times, last accessed 4 May 2014, http://thetehrantimes.tumblr.com/tagged/streetstyle.

148. Hamid Naficy, 'Veiled Vision/Powerful Presence: Women in Post-Revolutionary Iranian Cinema', in *Life and Art: The New Iranian Cinema*, ed. Rose Issa and Sheila Whitaker (London: NFT and BFI, 1999), 46–64.

149. 'Enforcement of Islamic Dress Code in Iran', *Iran News*, 9 August 2007, 00:03:23, last accessed 26 April 2014, http://www.youtube.com/watch?v=HgXgpngHf60.

150. Bucar, *Pious Fashion*, 55.

151. Masserat Amir-Ebrahimi, 'Transgression in Narration: The Lives of Iranian Women in Cyberspace', in 'Innovative Women: Unsung Pioneers of Social Change', special issue, *Journal of Middle East Women's Studies* 4, no. 3, (Fall 2008): 89.

152. Ibid., 93.

153. Chris Jenks, *Transgression* (London: Routledge, 2003), 8.

154. Ibid.

155. Milani, *Veils and Words*, 6.

156. Bucar, *Pious Fashion*, 30.

Appendix: The Showroom Project
September 2015

In September 2015, as part of a three-week public programme in collaboration with Louise Shelley at The Showroom London, I co-curated an installation of photographs by Hengameh Golestan from her *Women's Uprising* series on the events of 8 March 1979. The rest of the programme helped to unfold what happened on this day even further. For instance, we placed a table in the middle of the gallery to showcase books relating to the extensive research that had been conducted. The photographs varied in terms of

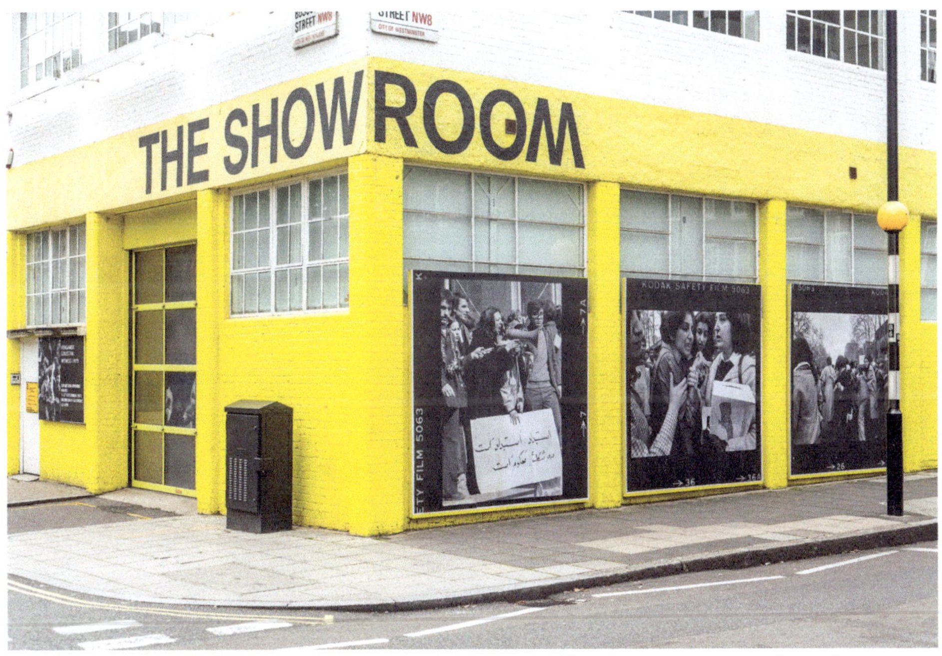

FIGURE 38: Dan Weill, documentation of *The Witness 1979*. The Showroom, London.

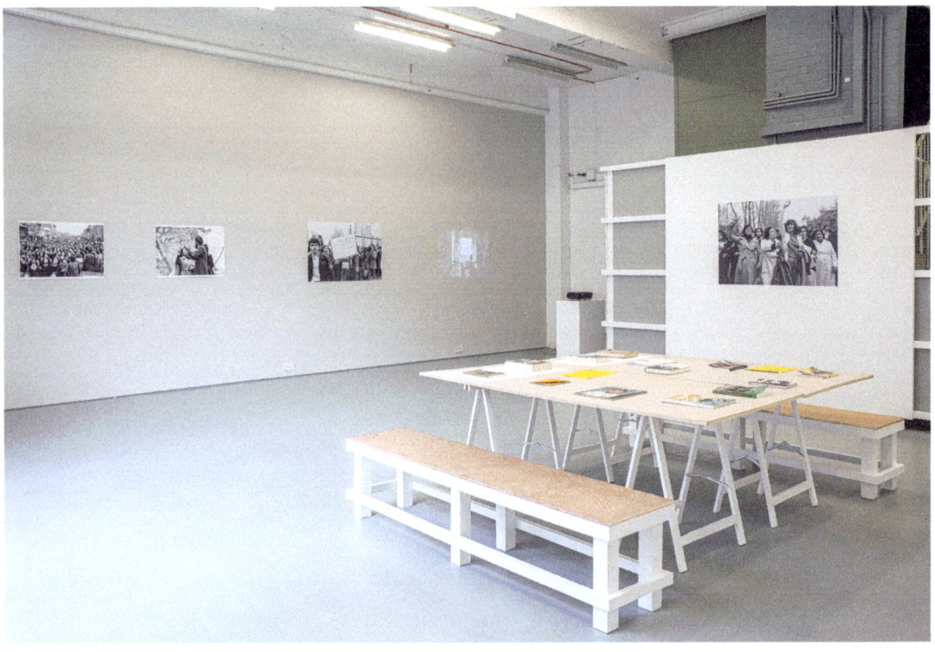

FIGURE 39: Dan Weill, documentation of *The Witness 1979*. The Showroom, London.

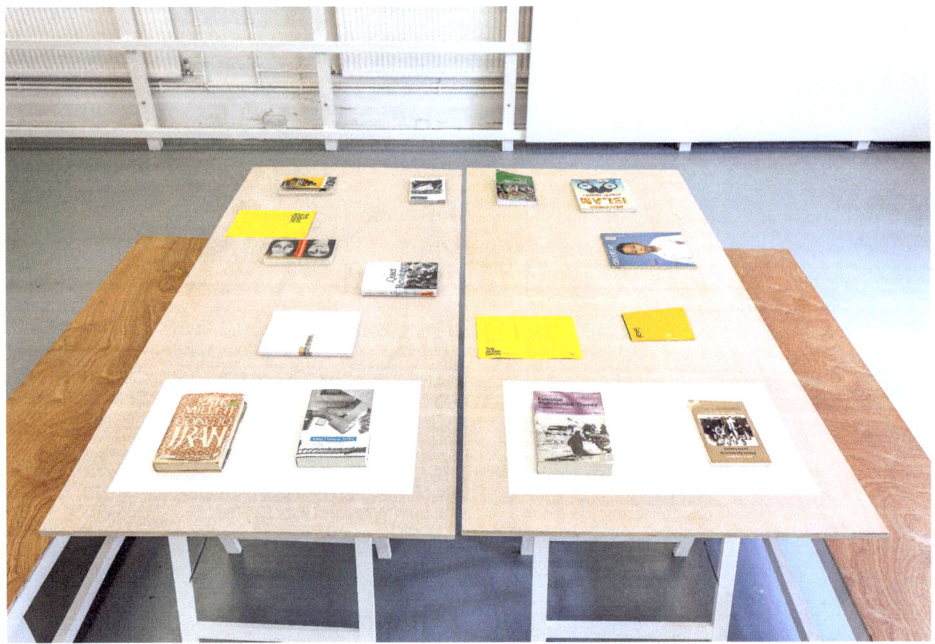

FIGURE 40: Dan Weill, documentation of *The Witness 1979*. The Showroom, London.

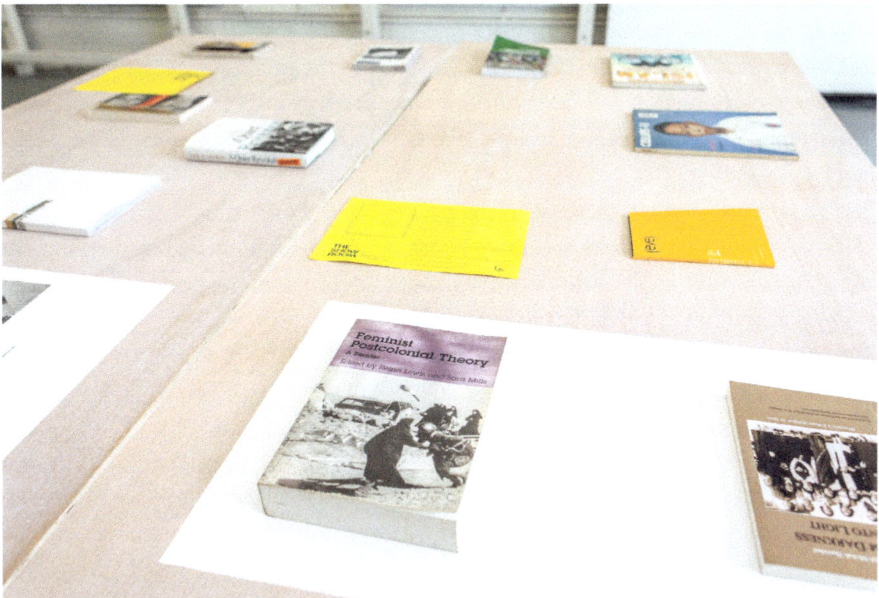

FIGURE 41: Dan Weill, documentation of *The Witness 1979*. The Showroom, London.

size and printing technique employed. We tried to use a mix of traditional fine art paper prints and vinyl prints; both were placed directly on the wall in the informal setting of The Showroom.

We used a projector to show twenty images on a loop; these were obtained from Golestan's archive during our meeting in Tehran in July 2015. The only video documentation of the 8th of March 1979 was shown on a single channel TV placed in the centre of the installation. Billboard-sized images were placed on the external walls of the gallery; these were life sized and could not be missed by anyone walking by – the streets of Tehran imposed on the streets of London.

It is important to note that The Showroom is not a white cube space but rather a platform for community work and discussion. It was a great chance to visually embody the space with the 8th of March 1979 uprising images and allow the atmosphere to develop naturally through different public activities, including screenings, a symposium and workshops, covering the theoretical aspects of the works, as well as the visual experimentation behind them.

Reflection on the Symposium

The two-day symposium was held at The Showroom on 5 and 19 September 2015.

On the first day Reina Lewis, professor of cultural studies at London College of Fashion (LCF), University of the Arts London (UAL), spoke of the politics of the veil and the politics of representation while reflecting on Golestan's photographs. Lewis noted: 'Hengameh works documenting women's life in Iran in the spectacular mode of public demonstration or in the quiet setting of everyday/domestic life, highlighting the way in which private feeds public and time and space merge into one another'. Lewis continued by explaining that the Women's Uprising of 1979 was not against veiling itself but rather against the imposition of the state's control over a woman's body; women demonstrated to preserve their autonomy, equal rights and independent choices.

Lewis' research on Muslim fashion, women, veiling and religious dress in a way validates the practice of veiling, while in the context of my own work, veiling is a representation of an autocratic political and religious stance to which I am opposed.

Sandra Schäfer was the second speaker; her book was the starting point of my Ph.D. research in 2011. During her presentation, Schäfer introduced a re-reading of the events of 1979 and, in particular, the Iranian Revolution, starting by discussing the way in which many political parties united to start the revolution. Schäfer noted that history is not linear and national but rather fragmented and trans-geographical. She showed a few short clips from her film *On the Set of Kabul/Teheran 1979ff* (2011)[157] while presenting her paper. Her narrative followed the questions: 'Where does a revolution start?' and 'where does it end?', if there even is an end. Schäfer is interested in the role of the micro-politics of the media and the way in which the events of 8 March 1979 were heavily covered in Germany and Turkey, but largely ignored by national Iranian television, although news and photos of the protest did appear in the print media for two weeks.

She spoke more generally about photographic representation by way of Hengameh's photographs. She noted: 'The people in Hengameh's photographs speak to me through their gestures and presence'.

The gestures and gazes of the women and the interactions between them speak to the viewer. This kind of communication between photograph and viewer Ariella Azoulay calls a 'civil contract' whereby the people in the photo and their gestures essentially enable a 'space' through which to communicate with the unknown public.[158] Golestan's photographs capture a moment of heightened protest, anger, pride, confidence and violence and also moments of negotiation.

The programme continued with a discussion between Golestan and myself in which I asked her about her experience during the uprising, her photographs and the way in which she has continued to work on this topic.

Golestan described hers as an unusual career for a woman since people were not used to seeing women photographers. There were, indeed, only a few women photographers in Iran at that time, including Maryam Zandi and Rana Javadi. Photography was considered more of a hobby then, and it would have been difficult for women photographers to obtain permission to cover conflicts from the authority. Today, women photographers are, of course, educated at university, and are highly skilled in technical aspects of documentary photography and journalism.

'I was 27 years old myself when the Revolution took place', Golestan said. 'Independence and freedom was the main theme of the Revolution. The protest was not against religion but rather about human rights and freedom of choice. As we can see, many women from religions other than Islam participated'. One woman at the demonstration can be seen in the short video shown at the exhibition explaining, 'I'm here for my 6 year old daughter, to protect her rights, not my own. In fact, I like to wear the veil but I want my daughter to be free to choose what she wishes'.

On the second day of the symposium Ziba Mir-Hosseini brought to our attention the relation between Islamic fundamentalism and women's rights in Iranian society. She talked about the development of the Islamic regime in the years after the revolution, noting the instrumental use of religion by the state to justify its autocratic rule in post-revolutionary Iran. She believes that this domestication was the main reason that the Green Movement was born in 2009, which brought about a new voice that combined the ethics of care and love with the ethics of justice and equality; above all, she said, this is the voice that rests on the promise of non-violence. She continued by saying that democracy and patriarchy are incompatible.

On the other hand, Shahin Nawai, one of the founding members of the National Unity of Women's Associations, which emerged during the Women's Uprising, brought to the table her own insight into the feminist movement during this era and the difficulties and challenges that it faced. She started her presentation by outlining the history of feminism in Iran from the early twentieth century, and expanding on the chronological description of Iranian women's achievements and the awakening of society.

After the victory of the revolution, there were four women's meetings announced at Tehran University, Nawai explained, which were all affiliated to different political parties. Nawai was not interested in any of them, as she was looking for an independent women's group. One day in late February 1979, she saw an advertisement on a noticeboard at the university expressing interest in starting such an organization. She attended the meeting and, together with the four women she met there, she established the National Unity of Women's Associations. A few weeks later, on the 8th of March 1979, the Women's Uprising happened and the National Unity of Women's Associations increased its activities and started to print flyers and distribute them among the demonstrators inviting them to meet or join, in order to engage in further discussions and actions.

Nawai noted the difficulties that women faced during the uprising since they had no support from political parties. Nawai explained,

> So by continuing the movement, we [the National Unity of Women's Associations]
> became isolated. We didn't have any supporters, not even from the left. On the other
> hand, many secular young students came and protected us through the demonstration
> and supported us in our fight for our rights.

What does this new representation present for me? Not just in terms of my research and Hengameh's works, but also with regard to the large network I have now established from the media and wider community. The aesthetic property of the work does not lie with the materiality of the project but rather with the social struggle it represents. The new stage of the project is solidarity; expanding on it in this way creates a larger understanding of this missing part of Iranian history and the events of 8 March 1979.

I thought back to my first encounter with Hengameh's photograph of 8 March 1979 at that book launch in London, which sparked my desire to want to know more about the image and the history behind it. In order to do so, I chose to do a research degree in the institutional framework of a western art school, the Royal College of Art, that allowed me to focus wholly on researching and articulating representations of this history through writing and making my own images. As I came to the end of my studies at the RCA, I returned to Hengameh's photograph in the context of a collaboration with The Showroom – a publicly funded community space that made it possible for me to take my own research out of the ivory tower of the art school into a public context more appropriate to an engagement with the unique historical document that the photograph had become.

The programme was covered by international media such as the *Guardian*, the *New York Times*, the *British Journal of Photography*, CNN and Euronews, and the attention brought the exhibited images to a much wider audience. On this occasion, the exhibition was not just an exhibition, but rather a place of research, and an opportunity to bring different views together to better map a significant historical event. The exhibiting of the photographs was, therefore, a mere staging, which allowed other things to happen. By staging the project, we created a new image, collectively and communally. This new image allows a new imagining to take place – an image of elsewhere – and that is, indeed, the quality of the revolutionary moment, the quality of imagining something else taking place. There is a new larger world that has been created around my research project, which may continue to expand. It is no longer just Hengameh, The Showroom and I, but rather a much larger group of people (the public).

NOTES

157. Sandra Schäfer, installation of 2-channel-video, duration 58, Germany, 2011.

158. Ariela Azoulay, *The Civil Contract of Photography* (Cambridge: MIT Press, 2012), 18.

Bibliography

Books and Articles

Amanat, Abbas, ed. *Taj Al-Saltana: Crowning Anguish: Memories of a Persian Princess from the Harem to Modernity 1884–1914*. Translated by Anna Vanzan and Amin Neshati. Washington, DC: Mage Publishers, 2003.

Amir-Ebrahimi, Masserat. 'Transgression in Narration: The Lives of Iranian Women in Cyberspace'. In 'Innovative Women: Unsung Pioneers of Social Change', special issue, *Journal of Middle East Women's Studies* 4, no. 3 (Fall 2008): 80–118.

Arendt, Hannah. *The Origins of Totalitarianism*. London: Penguin Books, 1951.

———. *On Revolution*. London: Penguin Books, 1963.

Azoulay, Ariela. *The Civil Contract of Photography*. Cambridge: MIT Press, 2012.

Badran, Margot and Cooke, Miriam. *Opening the Gates: A Century of Arab Feminist Writing*. London: Virago, 1990.

Bamdad, Badr ol-Moluk and Rahimieh, Nasin. *From Darkness into Light: Women's Emancipation in Iran*. Costa Mesa: Mazda Publishers, 1980.

Behdad, Ali. 'The Orientalist Photograph'. In *Photography's Orientalism: New Essays on Colonial Representation*, edited by Ali Behdad and Luke Gartlan, 33–46. Los Angeles: Getty Publications, 2013.

Benjamin, Walter and Arendt, Hannah. *Illuminations: Theses on the Philosophy of History*. Translated by Harry Zohn. London: Schocken Books, 1969.

Brookshaw, Dominic Parviz and Rahimieh, Naser. *Forough Faroukhzad: Poet of Modern Iran*. London: I.B. Tauris, 2010.

Bucar, Elizabeth. *Pious Fashion: How Muslim Women Dress*. Cambridge: Harvard University Press, 2017.

Bullock, Katherine. *Rethinking Muslim Women and the Veil: Challenging Historical and Modern Stereotypes*. Herndon: International Institute of Islamic Thought, 2007.

Carr, James. *Experiences of Islamophobia: Living with Racism in the Neoliberal Era*. London: Routledge, 2015.

Cixous, Hélène and Derrida, Jacques. *Veils: Cultural Memory in the Present*. Palo Alto: Stanford University Press, 2001.

Colomina, Beatriz. *Privacy and Publicity: Modern Architecture as Mass Media*. London: MIT Press, 1996.

Copjec, Joan. 'The Object-Gaze: Shame, Hijab, Cinema'. *Filozofski Vestnik* XXVII, no. 2 (2006): 24–27.

Craik, Jennifer. *Fashion: The Key Concepts*. Oxford: Berg, 2009.

Dabashi, Hamid. *Close Up: Iranian Cinema, Past, Present and Future*. New York: Verso, 2001.

Daneshvar, Simin. *Savushun*. Tehran: Alborz Publishing, 1969.

Daragahi, Haideh and Witoszek, Nina. 'Anti-Totalitarian Feminism? Civic Resistance in Iran'. In *Civil Society in the Age of Monitory Democracy*, Studies on Civil Society, edited by Lars Trägårdh, Nina Witoszek and Bron Taylor, 231–54. Oxford: Berghahn Books, 2013.

Doy, Gen. *Drapery: Classicism and Barbarism in Visual Culture*. London: I.B. Tauris, 2001.

Fanon, Frantz. *A Dying Colonialism*. New York: Grove Press, 1967.

Farrokhzad, Forough. 'The Wind Will Carry Us'. In *Another Birth*, translated by Ahmad Karimi Hakkak. Toronto: Mage Publishers, 1953. Last accessed 20 September 2015. http://www. forughfarrokhzad.org/selectedworks/selectedworks1.php.

Hadimioglu, Çagla. 'Black Tent'. TEXT Revue. 2010. Last accessed 12 November 2015. http:// www.text-revue.net/revue/heft-8.

Hoodfar, Homa. *Return to the Veil: Personal Strategy and Public Participation in Egypt*. London: Routledge, 1991.

Jenks, Chris. *Transgression*. London: Routledge, 2003.

Khiabany, Gholam and Sreberny, Annabele. 'The Women's Press in Contemporary Iran: Engendering the Public Sphere', 47–62. In *Women and Media in the Middle East: Power Through Self-Expression*, edited by Naomi Sakr. London: I.B. Tauris, 2004.

Khosravi, Jasmin. *Zabān-i Zanān – The Voice of Women: The Life and Work of Ṣadīqa Daulatābādī (1882–1961)*. Berlin: Eb-Verlag, 2012. Extract in English from original German.

MacLeod, Arlene E. *Accommodating Protest: Working Women, the New Veiling, and Change in Cairo*. New York: Columbia University Press, 1993.

Matin, Mahnaz and Mohajer, Naser. *Iranian Women's Uprising March 8th 1979 Vol. I: Renaissance*. Cologne: Nuqṭa Publishing, 2010.

Milani, Farzaneh. *Veils and Words: The Emerging Voices of Iranian Women Writers*. New York: Syracuse University Press, 1992.

Moallem, Minoo. *Between Warrior Brother and Veiled Sister*. Berkeley: University of California Press, 2005.

Moaveni, Azadeh. *Lipstick Jihad: A Memoir of Growing up Iranian in America and American in Iran*. London: Public Affairs Publishing, 2006.

Motahhari, Morteza. *The Problem of Hijab*. Tehran: Basir Publication, 1986.

Naficy, Hamid. 'Veiled Vision/Powerful Presence: Women in Post-Revolutionary Iranian Cinema'. In *Life and Art: The New Iranian Cinema*, edited by Rose Issa and Sheila Whitaker, 46–64. London: NFT and BFI, 1999.

Naficy, Hamid. *A Social History of Iranian Cinema*. Vol. 4. London: Duke University Press, 2012.

Nafisi, Azar. *Reading Lolita in Tehran*. New York: Random House Inc., 2003.

———. *Things I've Been Silent About: Memories*. London: Penguin Random House, 2008.

Naghibi, Nima. *Rethinking Global Sisterhood: Western Feminism and Iran*. Minneapolis: University of Minnesota Press, 2007.

Nameghi, Khadijeh Mohammadi and Gonzalez, Carmen Perez. 'From Sitters to Photographers: Women in Photography from the Qajar Era to the 1930s'. In *History of Photography: The First Hundred Years of Iranian Photography*, 48–73. Vol. 37, no. 1. London: Routledge, 2013.

Neshat, Shirin. *Women of Allah*. New York: Distributed Art Pub Inc., 1999.

Omrani, Homeira Ranjbar. *Jameyat zanan* (*Women Association of Iran*). Tehran: Nazar Print, 2004.

Razi, Ali. *Tarih-I-Mofassal-I-Iran* (*The Complete History of Iran*). Tehran: Eghbal and Shorakae Publication, 1956.

Riches, Harriet. 'Shadow Sites'. *Afterimage* 40, no. 6 (May/June 2013): 27–32.

Sadr, Hamid Reza. *Iranian Cinema: A Political History*. London: I.B. Tauris, 2006.

Sartre, Jean-Paul. *Being and Nothingness*. Translated by Hazel Barnes. New York: Washington Square Press, 1993.

Schäfer, Sandra, Becker, Jochen and Bernstorff, Madeleine. *Kabul/Teheran 1979ff*. Berlin: b_books, 2006.

Schmid, Christian. 'Henry Lefebvre: Theory of the Production of Space Towards a Three Dimensional Dialectic'. In *Space, Difference, Everyday Life: Reading Henry Lefebvre*, edited by Kanishka Goonewardena, Stefan Kipfer, Richard Milgrom and Christian Schmid, 27–30. London: Routledge, 2008.

Shayegan, Driush. *Asiya Dar Barabar Gharb* (*Asia Confronting the West*). Tehran: Amir Kabir Publishing, 1977.

Wiggins, Colin. *Alison Watt: Phantom*. London: National Gallery, 2008.

Media

'About Women's Organisation of Iran'. Women's Organisation of Iran. Last modified 20 April 2014. http://fis-iran.org/en/women/organization.

'Anthropology Museum of Quai Branly in Paris'. De Clérambault's work. Last accessed 1 October 2015. http://collections.quaibranly.fr/#0bf65ffc-9f7b-414d-81e1-a8ef93292c83.

'Enforcement of Islamic Dress Code in Iran'. *Iran News*. 9 August 2007, 00:03:23. Last accessed 26 April 2014. http://www.youtube.com/watch?v=HgXgpngHf60.

'Hidden Pearls'. Islam Great Religion. Last modified 4 December 2010. https://islamgreatreligion. wordpress.com/2010/12/04/hidden-pearls/.

'History of Photography in Iran'. The Freer|Sackler. Last accessed 20 April 2014. https://www. asia.si.edu/iran-in-photographs/intro-photography.asp.

'I Feel Sorry for the Garden'. Farrokhzad's Early Poems. Last modified 4 May 2004. http:// wordswithoutborders.org/article/i-pity-the-garden#ixzz3Zegnv1fN.

'Introduction to Women's Organisation of Iran'. Women's Organisation of Iran. Last modified 20 April 2014. http://fisiran.org/en/women/organization/introduction.

'Islamic Rules of Modesty for Women'. Quran Surat al-Nur Verse 31. Last modified 28 September 2015. http://quran.com/24/31.

Moulder, Michele, Boiasuna, Sylvia, Mular, Claudine and Rey, Sylven. 'The Only Video Evidence of That Historical Moment'. YouTube. Last modified 20 April 2015. https://www.youtube. com/watch?v=ulJwXHji6f4.

Nawai, Shahin. 'Le Comité des Femmes Contre la Lapidation, Paris'. 8 March 2015. Video, 01:01:49. https://www.youtube.com/watch?v=_7mnB_exy9I.

'Tehran's Street Styles'. The Tehran Times. Last accessed 4 May 2014. http://thetehrantimes. tumblr.com/tagged/streetstyle.

'The Post-Revolutionary Women's Uprising of March 1979: An Interview with Nasser Mohajer and Mahnaz Matin'. Iran Wire. Last accessed 12 October 2015. http://en.iranwire.com/ features/944/.

'The Women's Organization of Iran: Evolutionary Politics and Revolutionary Change', Women's Organisation of Iran. Last accessed 30 April 2019. http://fis-iran.org/en/women/ organization.

Movies

Bani-E'temad, Rakhshan. *Off Limits* (Kharej az Mahdudeh). Iran: Filmsazan Cooperation, 1986.

——. *Narges*. Iran: Arman Films, 1992.

Hekmat, Manijeh. *Women's Prison (Zendān-e Zanān)*. Iran: Bamdad Film, 2002.

Kiarostami, Abbas. *The Wind Will Carry Us*. DVD. France: MK2 Production, 1999.

Makhmalbaf, Mohsen. *Kandahar*. DVD. France: NBC Ajans [tr], 2001.

Milani, Tahmineh. *Two Women (Do zan)*. Iran: Arman Film, 2009.

Neshat, Shirin and Azari, Shoja. *Women Without Men*. DVD. USA: IndiePix Films, 2009.

Pratique, Politique et Psychanalyse (Michele Moulder, Sylvia Boiasuna, Claudine Mular and Sylven Rey). *Mouvement de Libération des Femmes Iraniennes: Année Zéro*. France,1979. YouTube. Last modified 20 April 2015. https://www.youtube.com/watch?v=ulJwXHji6f4.

Satrapi, Marjane and Paronnaud, Vincent. *Persepolis*. DVD. France: Celluloid Dreams, 2000.

Schäfer, Sandra. Installation of 2-channel-video, duration 58. Germany, 2011.

Acknowledgements

This publication has become possible with the generous support of Cathy Johns, Ezzidin Alwan, Fran Lloyd, Francette Pacteau, Hengameh Golestan, John Cussans, Juan Cruz, Naomi Curston, Michael Turco, Ros Murray, Stephen Atkinson, Stephen Barber, Touraj Atabaki and The Visual and Material Culture Research Centre, Kingston University, London.

Index

components, 41

compulsory, ix, xi–xii, 1, 9, 11–13, 17, 28, 32, 76

compulsory dress code, ix, xii, 1, 9, 12–13, 32, 76

concealment, 29

condemning, xii

confine, 2, 5, 19, 29, 58

Congress of the International Woman Suffrage Alliance, 8

Constitutional Revolution, 6, 20

constrict, 66

consumerist, 21, 28

controlling the look, 40, 42

covering, viii–ix, xi–xii, 1, 3–5, 9–11, 13, 15, 17–18, 29–31, 37, 41–42, 51, 54–55, 60, 74–76, 78, 87

cowboy style, 31

crumpled, 65

cultural backwardness, 5

cultural barriers, 28

cultural centres (*marakeze refahe khanevade*), 15

curve, 49, 61, 65, 69, 72

custom, 10, 30, 35

D

daguerreotype, 18–19

Dar al-Funun, 19

democracy, xiii, 22, 89

demonstration, xi, 12–13, 16, 88–89

dilemma, 80

disillusioned, 28

disintegrating, 27–28

displacement, 66

dissolves, 56, 61

distinction, 31

domestic, xii, 3, 26, 37–38, 57, 81, 88–89

double-edged, 30

drapery, 51, 66, 70–71, 82

drapes, 66

dress code, viii–ix, xii, 1, 2, 9–13, 21, 32, 74–76, 78, 80–81, 83

dull, 5

dwelling, 55

E

economic upheaval, 25

educated women, 1–2, 5–6, 13, 89

embodying, 69, 74

empowerment, 31, 39

enfolded, 29

enforcement, xii, 2, 4, 10–12, 76, 83

enlightened women, 2, 6

enlightenment goals, 5

espouse, 72

exposure, 29, 78

extra-diegetic, 37

F

fabric, 3, 10, 21, 30, 49, 54–55, 63, 66, 68–69, 72–73, 75

families (tradition), 30

Family Protection Act, xi, 1, 5, 9, 11, 31

fatwa (a legal opinion), 4

fear, 1, 5, 28, 46, 56

feeble, 5

female gaze, 21

feminism, viii–ix, xii–xiv, 5, 12, 17, 22, 24, 45, 89

fiction, 9, 25

fitna, 11

fitted, 74

flexion, 66

folds, 52, 55, 66, 69, 72, 75

forbidden, 37–39, 51–52, 54, 55

forcibly uncovered, 2

foreign, 35, 56

forgotten archives, viii

forlorn, 27

post-revolutionary, 10, 16, 24, 37–38, 45, 55, 76, 83, 89

practice-based research, viii

Pratique, Politique et Psychanalyse, xi, xiii, 12, 23

premodern, 61

presence, 6, 11, 21, 25, 28, 30, 36–38, 40–41, 45, 47, 56, 66, 68–69, 73, 75, 81, 83, 88

pride, 88

privacy, ix, 36–37, 44, 47, 51

private parts, 11, 39, 47, 75

public domain, 3, 8, 25, 29

public sphere, 10, 22, 29, 55, 80, 87

pushidan, 3

putridity, 27

Q

Qajar dynasty, 3, 5, 21

quotidian, 55

R

radical attitude of Islamic fundamentalism, 10

re-interpretation, 37, 58, 74

reform, xi, 4, 6, 14, 17, 55

regime, ix, xi, 16, 55–56, 76, 89

religious, 4, 6, 10, 17–20, 26, 28–29, 31, 39, 41, 55, 68, 78, 80, 88

religious piety, 28

renders, 44

repealed, xi

resistance, viii, xiii, 17, 22, 49, 76, 80

revolution, viii, xi–xii, 9–11, 16–18, 37–38, 55–56, 76, 81, 83, 89

revolutionaries, 9

revolutionary guards, xi

Reza Shah, xi, 1–5, 9–10, 17, 26, 55, 80

rusari ('headscarf'), 2, 32

S

Sadighe Dowlatabadi, 1, 6–8

salt-print, 19

Savushun, 25–26, 45

Sazman-e Basij-e Mostaz'afan, 76

scene, 33, 36–38, 49, 52, 54, 59–61, 65

schematic, 66

scopophilia, 41

scrutinized, 60

secret space, 40, 55, 63

secular fashion, 76

secularizing, xi

seduction, 34, 36, 41

segregation, 10, 29–30, 39

self-disparagement, 5

self-duality, 29–30

semi-private spaces, 55

sense of protection, 29, 31, 36, 42

sepia-toned, 21, 66

servile, 5

servitude, 57

sexual tension, 10–11, 74, 80

'Shahnameh', 28

shame, 4, 36, 40–41, 46, 78

Sharia law, 5

sharm, 4

Shiraz, 26

silk crepe, 31

sleek black oil, 72

slogans, 12

sloppy dress, 78

social classes, 6, 25

social status, 3–4, 6, 18

socializing, 55

socially produced, 52

societies (authoritative power), 30

socio-economic, 19

soft-spoken, 4

Solidarity Committee (CIDF), 13–14

space, viii, 3, 10, 20, 23, 30, 36–38, 40, 42, 44, 51–52, 54–55, 58, 62–63, 66 68, 72, 74, 78, 80, 82–83, 87–88, 90